BEARING THE MASK

BEARING THE MASK

Southwestern Persona Poems

Poetry of the American Southwest — No. 2

Edited by Scott Wiggerman
& Cindy Huyser

Foreword by Carmen Tafolla

Dos Gatos Press
Albuquerque, New Mexico

Bearing the Mask:
Southwestern Persona Poems
© 2016, Dos Gatos Press
ISBN-13: 978-09840399-9-9
Library of Congress Control Number: 2016935472

All rights reserved. No part of this book may be reproduced in any form without prior permission from the publisher and the copyright owner, except by reviewers who wish to quote brief passages.

Bearing the Mask is the second in a series from Dos Gatos Press: Poetry of the American Southwest.

First Edition:
16 17 18 19 20 21 22 5 4 3 2

Cover Art:
© *We'wha of Zuni*, Robert Lentz, OFM, Courtesy of Trinity Stores, www.trinitystores.com, 800.699.4482
robertlentz.com

Cover Design: David Meischen and Scott Wiggerman

Dos Gatos Press
6452 Kola Ct. NW
Albuquerque, NM 87120
www.dosgatospress.org

Contents

Foreword — vi

**From the Dawn
(to 1502)** — 1

**European Intrusion
(1503–1848)** — 13

**Territories to Statehood
(1849–1918)** — 45

**To the End of the Millenium
(1919–1999)** — 107

**The Twenty-First Century
(2000–present)** — 169

Contributor Notes and Index — 200

Index of Personae — 212

Foreword

A unique glimpse at a special region known to some as borderlands, this anthology of persona poems gives articulate voice to the many peoples and periods that have made their mark on this scarred and sacred land of deserts and rivers, Indian petroglyphs and fifty-foot marionettes, haciendas and Air Force bases, this ground so varied in climate and culture but so unified in spirit. The spirit of this terra incognita fits its original definition as "unknown territory," for unknown also implies undefined and therefore unbound, open to interpretation. The reach of these voices is both global and personal. From "Years Following Her Death, Former Texas Slave Silvia King Speaks to a Kidnapped Nigerian Girl" to "Chester Nez Arriving at Guadalcanal, 1942," these are human voices in all their honesty and depth of caring. And they are not told from only one side of the fence.

The range of voices here is as beautiful and translucent as a rainbow. From Cochise to Calamity Jane, Navajo Code Talkers to Japanese internees, Devil Girl and Old Man Gloom, slaves and stunt pilots, Paiutes and migrant mothers, Annie Oakley and Georgia O'Keeffe, security officers and French tourists, Gregorio Cortez, La Llorona, and Cynthia Ann Parker — all come to life here, speak their own truths and their own sacred space in these poems. The beauty of their lives shines through in a history that refuses to be erased, voices that refuse to be silenced. Such is the nature of persona poems drawn from the broad stroke of human experience. Even the buildings refuse to be quiet, as the infamous Phoenix Indian School whispers its evil tales and the Loretto Chapel staircase secretly smiles at its miracle. The very vividness of this book is that its personae, like the rainbow of individuals who have called this region home, span the full gamut and speak with such clear and haunting voices. To have them gathered in one assembly, so to speak, where one can, in a matter of hours, speak with Hoodoo Brown and Santa Teresa de Urrea, a Zuni Two-Spirit and a children's rights campaigner, a Crypto-Jew and a soldadera, a society patron and a stripper, appears to be a breathtakingly fortuitous opportunity.

But what stands out most about this volume is its broader vision and inclusion of the nations that came to this place before the planting of possessive flags. Unlike more conventional (and stereotypic) anthologies that suffer a persistent and stubborn Eurocentrism and worse, Anglocentrism, counting the beginning of all histories to be "when the white man arrived," or in the Southwestern version, since the U.S. English speakers arrived, *Bearing the Mask* has charged courageously into the times "before" — before European arrival, before traditional histories, before the conventional and boring canon of well-accepted facts that are so frequently repeated they often go unchallenged in their cultural bias. Here, both the legendary heroes and the everyday working people of a pre-Columbian "Southwest" are represented, and their statements are as rich and singular and vital to our choir of voices as those of any tenor or celebrity. Even the green anole and the orb spider have their voices in this Southwest, this world before European invasion. And what follows does not disappoint. We have met a whole village of people here, spanning centuries, races, professions, and sexual identities. And arching over all these individuals, each stunningly handsome in the rawness of their vivid confessions, graceful in the depth of their driving force, lies the connecting spirit of this land, this place that holds their souls and buries their bones. Ultimately, this volume becomes a tribute to the magic present in this dust, the voices singing from these trees, the sense of place that lets one hear and touch and celebrate the many lives still breathing on this wind, beside us.

Singular for its balance and its stance against inhumanities like racism and sexism, this anthology keeps a truly holistic perspective on what this region emanates in its spirit, its courage, and its beauty. This is one of the most unique, diverse, and authentically exciting portrayals of the voices of the Southwest I have seen because it has told the many sides of the story and plumbed the many layers of history, taking us beyond our own shallow and thin-voiced prejudices and into the fullness of a rich and powerful harmony of many varied songs of human experience.

Carmen Tafolla
State Poet Laureate of Texas 2015-2016

From the Dawn (to 1502)

Creatures of Imagination

I. Anole

All afternoon
and into the early evening
I march up and down
the long trunk
of the rough oak.
The pink pulse of my dewlap
lifts and sets the sun.
My skin is the envy of avocados.

II. Polyphemus Moth

I emerge from my sac
of brown silk

plumose antennae tremble
in an air of perfumes

I am the world
at its beginning

    Mobi Warren

I step into my backyard and within minutes am mesmerized by the many-layered world of creatures who are the original inhabitants of this land, present long before we were. We live within their ancient rhythms; they awaken our imagination.

Yanaguana, Payaya woman/spirit

Yanaguana Reflects on the Yanaguana River

Though I can chant deep
as the trembling roar of the earth
under buffalo hooves reshaping the hills
Though I can dance in swift twirls and sing
to the purple heavens, my ringing voice as loud as
the chachalaca's yodeling of the coming chubasco
all drumming thunder and winds of change
Though I have had my lightning moments
of words slicing air
straight as a hand-carved arrow, yet —

I know how to silence my soul till time stands as one body
all here, all mine, all embracing,
I know how to dreamvision what has come before me
and some of what is yet to be.

You see, those moments are still vivid.
Those many days searching for water,
crawling through the dust, tongue thick with thirst,
taste of blood inside my lungs
scorched sun inside my eyes . . .

Till I saw, bursting from the earth, from that blue hole of spirit waters,
the waterbird, Anhinga, spreading wings that shed
cool droplets on the earth
and planted life.

In those still moments between my life and death,
too weak to move, too dry to breathe,
I saw the panther — blue as a jewel — swim in this hole of wonders
then spring like dawn and bless the drumbeat of this place with
his slow saunter, as a rippling river sprouted from this sacred hole.
And I chose transformation. Rebirth.
Chose to wed my spirit joyously to his life-giving playful dance,
to keep us always smoothly moving full of grace,
to keep us flowing always, like this river,

connected to what's come before
and to what lies ahead

And I, a woman still, though now in spirit ripples, in and out and
       harmonized,
find my heart moved to silence
stillness
hearing the whispered echo of
eternity
against this aqua sky dotted
  with white bursts of happiness
against the lush canopy of trees
  that guard this sacred place
against the flow of people that
  were here before us
  and will, surely, follow, rippling laughter,
  after we are gone

This silence I bequeath you
this ribbon of silent waters
this ribbon
that has already
quietly
stolen our
souls

    Carmen Tafolla

Yanaguana, lost in the scorched land and searching for water, weak, dizzied and near death, heard the Mother Earth remind her that she need only ask for help and She would protect her. Just then, an anhinga burst from a deep blue hole in the earth, from whence sprung cool, life-giving waters. Droplets slipped off its wings, fell to the earth, and brought life. Too weak to survive, Yanaguana chose to become a spirit in the water, watching the people grow from the quiet green river that sprung there. The settlement became known by the same name as the river, Yanaguana ("silent spirit waters"), today known as San Antonio.

chubasco: storm

Tlochtli player (circa 600-900)

Ballplayer Before the Ritual Game

Ahead —
the game.
A dance of destined grace
A God's awakening of spirit strength
A labored prayer of life's final sport

This is the equinox
My life at highest bloom
And then the sun goes out
the spirit leaves my eyes
the fast hot wind of game
departs my lungs
with not a tiniest glance back
It turns its face and leaves.

I'll miss the ball
the breath of life
the wind of speed
the joy of life's full effort

Ahead —
the game
a dance
my life

    Carmen Tafolla

Similar to basketball, the game of tlochtli was played by two teams with a rubber ball that was shot through a stone ring on the side walls of the court. In larger cities, custom often had the athletes treated royally, and the losing team was ceremonially executed. Most popular in Mexico Tenochtitlan and the interior of present-day Mexico, tlochtli courts have been found as far north as Flagstaff, Arizona, where ruins of a tlochtli court can be seen at Wupatki National Monument.

Hopi cotton picker/weaver (circa 1000)

El Piscador

Here in my furrow
i see the worms
enter the cotton-fruit
and kiss their inexperienced lips.

Sitting here
i feel the wind
whipping my face
to extract my sweat.

The faces of the cotton plants
patiently wait
for my hands to pull out
their white eyes
stuffing them in the sack.

And the black cat
waits for the sun to sleep.

    Armando P. Ibáñez

Cotton has been cultivated in the Southwest by the Hopi for over a thousand years, an important crop for the weaving and fiber arts still practiced in pueblos across the Southwest.

El Piscador: The Harvester

Corn Maidens, Hopi legend

Lesson of the Corn Maidens

we showed them what was right
        to eat
gave them each
a kernel to nurture
kept them
from poisoning themselves
showed them how much
they were loved

the men thought why not
tried to take us too

we have always been taken
        for granted

so we became mist
learned how to disguise ourselves
learned it is best to hide

we taught this lesson to our daughters

isn't it better this way?

    Jennifer Smith

There are many variants on the story of the Corn Maidens, but I always found the key points to be that these bringers of corn had to be turned to mists so that the men, who did not value and respect them as they should have, could not get to them. It was the women who had to disappear.

Ancestral Puebloan potter (circa 200-1300)

Potter at Chaco

The white clay slick beneath my palms,
I shape a jar in which to store precious water
so scarce in these times of drought
that draw the People tight within our canyon.

From this narrow cliffside terrace
I see smoke wreathing from a kiva,
just as our ancestors emerged from their sipapu,
fleeing the Underworld to shape a homeland.

Their spirits take my hands now, guide them
as the vessel spirals thin and tall.
Once heat has baked it hard, I will add sacred designs
to honor them — angles and turns ineffable as their wisdom.

Then my husband — our wares nestled
in a net upon his sturdy back—will bear it up
the Great North Road, trading in a village far away
for food, perhaps a lovely stone or feather, too.

Somewhere, days hence, unknown lips
will receive a gift of cool and vital water
from my distant, thoughtful fingers,
kiss the edges I now taper.

    David Bowles

The potter was a key figure among the Ancestral Puebloans who lived over a large part of the Four Corners area of the Southwest. The Ancestral Puebloans (once known as the Anasazi) had an indelible cultural and religious impact with their unique cliffside architecture, such as at Chaco Canyon, and their heavily adorned pottery.

sipapu: a small hole in the floor of a kiva

Ancestral Puebloan women, Mesa Verde (circa 1300)

Last Day

Clouds came once more today, sky dark
and heavy with rain that does not reach us.

Clouds rumble and swell. Clouds let go
the water they hold. We watch the rain

come down. But the day is parched.
We watch the falling fade. Rain does not

reach the earth we tend. The day drinks
every drop. And our hearts thirst. Our beans thirst.

Our squash and corn leaves wilt.
They do not blossom. They cannot feed us.

The wind sings to us
between our walls of rock.

We have packed what we can carry.
We leave behind the bones of grandmothers,

of children laden in our hearts.
Our home is here but we must go.

The shadows stretch and cool.
Tonight the moon reveals herself in full.

Tonight we follow the men.
They were gone searching and came

home. They tell of a stream
many days walking. They tell of water

rushing bank to bank. They tell
of deer that fatten in the green.

Tonight we follow the men
We carry our lives to the water.

David Meischen

I was a child when drought came to the farm I called home. I saw what lack of rain can do to land expected to feed humans and their animals. I watched the women — my grandmother and other farm widows, my mother and her neighbors — making a life within the limits dryland farming dictated. These women were a study in endurance. Many years later, I walked among the ruins at Colorado's Mesa Verde National Park. At quiet places, I let go of the moment and listened. If I emptied myself of everything except waiting, I could hear voices from before. They were always the voices of women.

La Llorona, legendary ghost

The Song She Cries

The mud is calling you.

Mud, mud, mud.
There is nothing better
for cooling the blood.

My legacy will be
I can make anything
into a song.

The river is calling now.
I must push your body into it.

Blood, blood, blood.
There is nothing sweeter
to ripen the mud.

Amanda Chiado

La Llorona, also referred to as the Weeping Woman, comes to us as a legend of a homicidal and suicidal mother who exists as a phantasm in limbo between here and the afterlife. She has been associated with Cihuacoatl, the Aztec goddess of fertility and childbirth, whose distressed cries about the imminent destruction of her children have been said to presage the coming conquest.

European Intrusion (1503–1848)

García López de Cárdenas (circa 1540), Spanish conquistador

Garcia López de Cárdenas at the Grand Canyon

Did God carve this deep cathedral
as advice for the architects of Italy?
I count eight shades of red, bleeding

like crocus petals into the memories
of my men. We are so thirsty,
but the blue ribbon of water

is a distant thread pumping coolly
through the inaccessible valley below.
Perhaps this great seam swallowed

the seven cities of gold, along with
each sycamore tree's roots
that comb the striated edges

of the colorful canyon. There is nothing
to bring back as any kind of proof
that clouds blush in the presence

of such beauty, that hawks brake
in midair as shadows lengthen.
The moon yawns bright, its tenor

increasing in volume until the night
is simply a song echoing and echoing
in yet another unfamiliar language.

    Robert Wynne

García López de Cárdenas was a Spanish conquistador who was the first European to see the Grand Canyon.

Alonso del Castillo Maldonado (1500s), explorer

Child of the Sun

Tomorrow I will tell him this
is it.

I won't blow another sacred
breath. He will laugh (I've said it
twice before). Naked and sitting
in moonlight, spindly shins crossed,
he nods at me. He found his peyote.
Soon I will inhale his smoke and pray
that this burned girl before me
will rise from her bed, whole
and hungry, but then I'm done.

I will touch her face, brush her hair
off her scarred mouth and whisper
the Pater Noster in her ear. I will promise
her mother that God is here, in my heart,
in my lungs and on my tongue; that nothing
of this miracle is me. And she will say
something I can't understand. And
we all will dance and maybe get
to eat their meat.

But then I will tell him, no more.

He rubs his beard and nods again,
what am I waiting for? He doesn't
know my hollow heart, what I have done
for a bite of gristle, that I can't stop
stealing the whitest shells from his pouch,
or staring at these women's ochre breasts,
or wishing all of this holiness would end.

But I obey them both, our Lord and
this barefoot conquistador I trail
behind through seas of thorns. I bend
forward and exhale all I have onto
the babe's belly. And like all the others,
she stirs and asks for water. Her mother
shrieks and drops to her knees and fills
my hands full of pretty rocks. I pocket
them all. And he winks at me and laughs
and claps, and lifts one of my aching arms
to the stars.

Melissa Jones Brewer

Alonso del Castillo Maldonado was one of the four survivors of the Panfilo de Narváez expedition. He traveled the new land with Cabeza de Vaca, performing miracles with him and spreading the Christian faith among the Native Americans, until he decided he was no longer worthy of such work.

Álvar Núñez Cabeza de Vaca (1490–1558), explorer

Faith Healer

Once I removed an arrowhead
from a native's chest.
Thanks to our prayers
and the grace of our God
he survived.

When I was shipwrecked
naked and hungry
along this wretched coast
they fed me.
They clothed me.
I am learning their ways,
digging roots
— women's work —
to free their men for hunting.
I have become a trader
of shells, bows, arrows.

I am their beast of burden
their slave
their faith healer.

Once I was a soldier
appointed by the King of Spain
as chief officer
in the Narváez Florida expedition.
I am still an explorer.

At last I escape
with my three companions,
Dorantes, Castillo and Estevanico,
and venture on foot,
crossing rivers,

living with the Coahuilteca.
Finally we reach the other sea.
How far are we from Mexico City?

Marcelle H. Kasprowicz

Second in command of the Narváez Florida Expedition and one of its four survivors, Cabeza de Vaca traveled throughout the Southwest trading, living and working with the Native American Stone Age tribes. His resilience and resourcefulness were remarkable, and his anthropological accounts are considered uniquely important. Source: Cabeza de Vaca, La Relación.

The Turk (1500s), Native American slave and guide

Death Song of the Turk

They will come in the night, three strong men
with a rawhide rope, and I will be ended
where I began, near these small rivers
dividing the unending sweep and ripple of grasses
taller than a man. They will leave my bones
for the vultures, my name forgotten yet again:
as first by the Apaches who stole me away,
a boy searching for birds' eggs on these prairies;
next by the pueblo people who bought me
as a slave; then by the Spanish conquerors
who called me Turk after some enemy
in their other world beyond the waters.

It was my salvation and my curse
to understand their tongue, to fathom
their lust for treasure and to give them
the promises they so wished to hear:
golden cities to the east, myself the guide.
How else could I make my return, how else
lure them away and spare my own people
the fate of the pueblos? They never knew
of the warnings I sent ahead, the horses
I secretly released, the miles and days
I added to their journey, leading them away
from villages I knew. And now at last
Coronado wearies of the search, sends his army
back to the west, and in his failure
turns on me, the treacherous guide,
the disappointed hope, the fated sacrifice.

O my people of the winds and tall grasses,
your brother did not forget you;
the invaders turn back their horses
and you are safe for another season.

Yet they must have their riches
and they will return. Keep far away
from the gleam of their helmets, the fire
and thunder of their muskets. Do not befriend
the black-robed carriers of crosses
or the bleeding god to whom they bow.
O bison, O badger, O prairie grouse,
hide your habitations from those who come
to use you without care for your ways
then cast you off, as they have done
in my presence, as they now do to me.
I have seen the twilight that awaits;
know my sorrow, hear my warning,
that you may preserve the world we know
for some little time after I have gone.

    Michael Harty

"The Turk" was a Native American guide, probably of the Pawnee tribe, who in 1541 accompanied Coronado's expedition in search of the fabled Golden Cities of Cibola. Somewhere in the present state of Kansas, Coronado gave up the search, and before returning to New Mexico, ordered The Turk strangled.

Maria Isabel Romero (1600s), Conversa/Crypto-Jew

Los Secretos de Mi Abuelita

From a low branch, I watch
Abuelita's house as the sun
disappears on a Friday. Soft light
flickers behind closed curtains.

I want to ask about just-lit candles,
the bowl of water and herbs in her room
near a retablo of Santa Esterika,
what she and Madrecita use it for each month.

Why do we clean on Fridays, stop at sunset,
not wear yellow? Lines in Abuelita's face
are sculpted by what is hidden. Veiling
her true heart, devotion to El Dio: exhaustion —
the strain of keeping a gourd from breaking
into a thousand pieces, of knowing whether
to let the unrevealed be buried with her or pass
along the joy and burden to another generation.

Which road to follow when none is marked
by safety and the only certainty is risk?
The weight of our ancestral soul map. Standing
vigil next to fields of corn and squash,
the ordinariness of white sheets and petticoats
on a clothesline lend cover to any cracks
in her fachada. I do ask her why I love
Santo Moises but don't like to go to church.
Esta en la sangre, pobrecita, is all she will say.

Carol Alena Aronoff

---

fachada: façade; Esta en la sangre, pobrecita: It's in the blood, poor little one

Maria Isabel Romero (1600s), Conversa/Crypto-Jew

Remembering Mi Abuelo

The scar on La Culebra's belly runs
serpentine across the bloodstained
landscape, lightning rod for a woman's pain.

Behind closed curtains I helped stitch Abuelo's shroud
with prayers and silk thread then covered the mirrors.
Thick walls in my grandparents' house absorbed our sorrow.

As we mourned, we remembered: the sound of morning
prayers in the hidden room — a music to feed the neshama,
the laughing bells on Abuelo's horse, the light in his eyes.

His tears of rage when he told us of jackals and rogues
cloaked as friars who blackmailed his brothers with threats
of autos-da-fé, his tears of sorrow when his only son died.

I have come to La Culebra to honor Abuelo, to place
a stone on his grave, stones upon stones,
stars within crosses, a small open book of life.

At sunset, the hills are mauve and rough
carnelian; my children play and hide amidst
gravestones and garter snakes at the camposanto.

On moon-blessed evenings like this, when sage gleams
silver and sparrows surrender to sleep, I remember the family
stories he shared that kept us awake and determined to triumph.

Carol Alena Aronoff

La Culebra: harmless snake/mountain peak near San Luis; neshama: soul; camposanto: cemetery

Maria Isabel Romero (circa 1600s), Conversa/Crypto-Jew

Kaddish

Mi esposo wanders the mesa finding solace on the rim of moonless night.
Miguel, born of conquistadors, bears secrets whispered only in the night.

Along the Rio Grande, he hears the shofar of his ancestors calling him to pray.
Fragments of psalms passed through la sangre, he recites before bed each night.

How can he wear two faces without confusion or regret? Without giving himself away?
His heart is weighed down by the santos he turns toward the wall each night.

His neshama, veiled by piety, outward devotion to Catholic rite, longs to be free.
I offer him a continent of stars and succor, as we come together to love at night.

As rezador, he must guard the sacred texts, remember the proverbs and prayers.
He will stand with the men in a hidden room as they daven on Shabbos night.

During the day, he mingles, oil and water, with the trinity: culture, politics, religion.
Bird of prey, he must watch for snakes and scorpions, relaxing vigilance only at night.

Where is the grace in the Edict of Grace? Why does blood drip from wings of tolerance?
Miguel writes our history with his boot in the sand, cries out his sorrow to the night.

Eyes toward Jerusalem, he prays for a world he believes was meant to be.
Déjame morir y ser enterrado como un judío: his last words echo through the night.

Carol Alena Aronoff

Speaker in all three poems is a Conversa/Crypto-Jew named Isabel (Hebrew name Raquel) who lived in New Mexico with her family during the 1600's

kaddish: memorial prayer; shofar: ram's horn; la sangre: blood; neshama: soul; rezador: prayer leader; daven: pray; Shabbos: Sabbath; Déjame morir y ser enterrado como un judío: Let me die and be buried as a Jew

25

Chief Orejas de Conejo/Rabbit Ears (1700s), Native American leader

Chief Orejas de Conejo

Old Chief Winter, being hungry,
chomped off bits of my flesh,
and I took the name Rabbit Ears.
Like the rabbit, I hid in the tall grasses
by the mountain peaks and watched,
picking up dust from the wagons
with the tip of my tongue,
waiting, unseen and still,
for the sound of water splashing
the groaning wheels and snorting beasts,
men distracted by care of their charges.

Then, my braves beside me,
I leaped and pounced
in the long light, thumping my great feet
across the open grasslands,
tricking the invaders like Rabbit
fooled the Wolves, plundering
those fat wagons of their bounty,
then danced ever further away,
escaping again and again.

The old ones sang of the Rabbit,
clever and swift, trapped by wolves.
Rabbit offered to show the circling pack
a new dance with his mighty feet,
and the playful wolves howled with joy.
Rabbit danced ever closer to his meadow,
then — bounding up into the sky,
he darted through the tall grass
to his warm burrow. The great wolf
clawed at the entrance, but Rabbit
kicked his snout and he fled.

Like wolves, their army followed me,
scented me out in my burrow at dawn,
and when I stuck out my head,
split it with a Spaniard's silver sword.
They gave my name to the mountain
where they piled our skulls,
less tribute than warning:
tease the wolf, my sons, and you,
too, will feel his steely jaws.

Diana L. Conces

The twin peaks near the town of Clayton, NM, are named Rabbit Ears, after Chief Orejas de Conejo (Chief Rabbit Ears) of either the Cheyenne or Comanche (it's not certain which tribe). In retribution for his raids on wagon trains, the Spaniards led an army to his village and slaughtered the men.

Angelina (circa 1680–1729), Hasinai interpreter

Angelina Sees Father Damián Again

Padre, I had never met
a person so far from home.
Your eyes like scurrying beetles

afraid of bigger things,
afraid your god —
that pale sun —
would diffuse.

My tongue molded words
like hierba and fuego
but you did not tell me
words are the ghosts of real things.
Every time I spoke
white smoke poured from my mouth.

Did I blame you?

Only if you counted bodies.

The worst of the world
sank in your skin.
What could you do about that?
Keep your skin.

I grew, had children.

If a man came to me
with the ocean sloshing
between his ears
I did not stop to ask
the name of his god.

What grace I found
I found
in the open hand.

    Alana Torrez

Angelina was a Hasinai woman who assisted Spanish missionaries active in Texas during the late 17th and early 18th centuries. Written accounts from the Spanish and French provide only a few tantalizing bits of information: she left her village to learn Spanish at Mission San Juan Bautista, spent time mediating and interpreting for various parties, and helped save the life of a French officer. Damián Massanet was a Franciscan priest who in 1690 helped found San Bernardino de la Caldera in the area of Angelina's village. Some of his writing has survived in which he mentions Angelina, particularly her "bright intellect" and "striking appearance," in addition to noting her desire to learn Spanish..

Maria Ysidora Vigil (1809–1872), Hispano mountain man's partner

I Liked Gringos, and They Liked Me

I liked los gringos, and they liked me,
especially Julián Popé from Quinteque.
I remember his eyes like flint; his voice — the striker;

and I, his tinder nest during that kindling summer of 1826.
¡Ay! Mijita, María Dolores, erupted from our flame
the following spring. Dolores. Sorrows. *Natural* daughter

of love. Those gallinas de Taos laid gossip like eggs,
but everyone (including mi familia) was in that bed
of Americano traders and men of the mountains,

covered with lust to trade Chimayó blankets
and beaver pelts for better supplies, Pawnee cautivos,
and horses from someplace called California.

By Autumn 1827, another wild seed blossomed,
only days before Julián followed Snake River west
to an ocean I could not imagine. He was gone

when that priest would not write Julián's name on the ledger,
so I christened the baby Julianita and called her Popé.
His friends stood beside me. Some married mis comadres.

Extranjero stories, silver earrings to our ears.
Our fathers' land, our own ripe longing for marriage —
plucked fruit for them. I think back to that time,

before mi primo, Antonio, died and left a widow,
who married and widowed again, before netting my butterfly
and floating to Julián's California dream of owning land.

Yes, he came back to Taos, but that man had no shame —
He laughed off his arrest as a spy. I was no longer
enchanted with mariposa fantasies. Three years before

their vows, I married another, Don Miguel Antonio León.
My father's soul now can rest — Miguel honored
my daughters with his name. We still live in Taos,

but we laugh that three countries have passed through
our village in twenty-five years like winds from three armies
of heavenly-and-demon angels — Nueva España, México,

the United States of America. We still see bad omens behind eyes
of some compadres, bright like embers left from the Taos War.
Sometimes, we are not sure to whom we belong, and we talk

about moving north to Colorado. I am prima to the new governor,
Donaciano Vigil, though we are sorry Governor Bent is gone. ¡Dios Mío!
So many new graves! My eyes are empty of tears from too many velorios

within two full moons. My future, mi Julianita, is her father's child.
She married John Albert, scout for Kit Carson. None of us could
        pronounce
his name, so he was baptized Juan de Dios, a prophecy. God saved him

from Simeon Turley's burning mill, la destilería of Taos Lightning.
Our neighbors say its flames were fueled by breath of el diablo,
but I pay them no attention. I'll ask Juan to tell you the story.

    Karen S. Córdova

Written in the voice of Maria Ysidora Vigil of Taos, NM, partner of mountain man William Pope (called Julián Popé). The Spanish side of Ysidora's family was in New Mexico for over 200 years when she was born. I expect the Native American side (through her mother) had been there for thousands of years.

gallinas: chicken-hearted people; cautivos: captives; mis comadres: my women friends; extranjero: foreign; mi primo: my cousin; mariposa: butterfly; prima: cousin; velorios: wakes

John David Albert (1806–1899), mountain man

Screaming Shadows of Burning Men

Before I begin, take heed: To hear the whole story, you will be here for three moons. I danced for weeks with La Muerte, who leaned in for a kiss, and I ducked, before kicking her into blue changeling Rio Hondo, bruised darker than bitter ale. I wish I could never look back

upon the lunacy of those three weeks when dancing Death leaned in *. . . to the dark hours of that day and to my suffering in the days following dark bruising of Rio Hondo. Month of bitter ale. Even now, I never look back . . . but the devil gets in me bigger than a wolf.* Haunts even my skin.

Suffering hours still darken my days and, I fear, all my following days. From my farm, perched high on the mesa, you can see across the river. Tomorrow, when sun devil rises louder than howling wolf, haunts my skin, look yonder — northwest where Turley's Mill once ruled jagged

over everybody's farm and table. Whiskey high. You can see across the river the edge of a breaking nation, hear bullet moans of men, berserk, killing neighbors. Look yonder, north and west of Turley's once mill, toward the future. Jagged rule of outsiders like me will continue to suckle the breast of our new country.

We jumped the Mexicano ledge of a breaking nation, but berserk Taoseños
aimed to sever Manifest Destiny. Take your time. I'll boil coffee.
El niño will suckle Julianita's breast. Then, she'll make a country breakfast
while you spy on massacred remains — boulders charred with ashes

of severed destinies. Time aimed to manifest the taking of blood, boiled like coffee.
These were my compadres. Sometimes, I visit and hear death gurgles of ghosts.
While you spy on massacred remains on boulders — char and ashes —
imagine that night, last January. Winter. A bullet cut the brim of my hat.

I heard death gurgles of my compadres. Our last rendezvous. Ghosts visit me.
I ran from screaming shadows of burning men, but they continue to follow,
like winter bullets cut the brim of my hat. Imagine that January night.
Maybe, when our family moves to Colorado, their souls will rest. I'm leaving

shades of burning men next week. Will they continue to run after me, screaming?
Next week, I will scout for land near the Arkansas River. I told the priest,
so my soul could maybe rest. Before my family can move to Colorado, I'm leaving.
Padre Martinez will buy this farm. We can't stay in the bull's eye of 500 neighbors.

Karen S. Córdova

This poem, using a pantoum-like form, is in the voice of mountain man John David Albert, survivor of the Massacre at Turley's Mill and Distillery, Arroyo Hondo, New Mexico, January 1847.

Andrea Castañón Villanueva/Madam Candelaria (1785–1899), innkeeper

The *San Antonio Daily Light* Interviews Madam Candelaria in 1895

Sit right there at porch edge — right square
in front of me. I have outlived my ears.
I will need to see your mouth for questions.
So. I'll do my best but it was long ago.
No, my little perro will not bite.
Gordita she is, fat as the ones I served,
the Texians and Tejanos when they came
to my hotel to eat, to dance the fandango,
mingle, enjoy themselves. Who knew,
come six days later, they would all be dead?
Claro! I saw it all. Listen to me well
for they tell me I am one hundred and ten —
no one else is left. Mi cuento es doloroso
and it will be double in my heart if I learn
you wrote the wrong words in the news.

I was Andrea Castañón Villanueva. Still,
married to a Candelario, who could resist
being renamed? But this reminds me,
General Houston wrote me a note, called me
"Candelarita," said, "go to Bowie in the Alamo."
We all knew the situation was difícil, muy difícil,
noise for days — smoke and clamor, shouting.
What was to become of San Antonio de Béxar?
The messenger slipped through in the night,
knocking, then calling softly, "Ven rápido!"
I took a sack, filled it with aloe spears,
with manzanilla leaves, a jug of water,
soft rags, a piloncillo to sweeten the pain.
In a side room he was, poor man on a cot,
his face bright hot, his eyes a-glitter.
"Ah, Madam Candelaria, you have come,"
he said, and laid his head against me.
I put water to lips, a cool cloth to brow —
(Aieee! My own rheumy body pains me

as I think of his suffering — Here, Gordita,
sit on my feet — a little dog helps.)

I could hear gunshots, the Mexicanos' shouts
as they came near despite the pleas
of Travis to let a dying man alone. Pardon my tears —
they never cease to come when I tell this part:
such though he was, Bowie insisted on firing
his firearm, over and over, only to fall back,
entreating my help to reload. One last time,
and his body went slack in my arms.
The typhoid had claimed him. At once,
the Mexicanos burst into the room, coming at us
with their bayonets. "Por el amor de Dios,"
I screamed, "don't spoil a dead man's body!"

As they bore down on him — Come close —
they grazed me here — See the scar on my face?
No? I assure you it is no wrinkle of age.
I've borne it 59 years. Wait, I'll wipe my tears —
I'll stand, lean over toward you . . . Right there . . .
Um hunh . . . you see? And while I'm standing,
you are welcome to drop a coin or two
into the pocket of this old apron I always wear.

Thank you, and send your friends around.
I can tell this saddest of stories many ways.

Jan Seale

Madam Candelaria, an innkeeper in San Antonio at the time of the battle at the Alamo, is thought to have been brought into the Alamo when it was under siege in order to nurse James Bowie, ill with a fever. She lived to be 113 and told her story in lively drama to tourists and journalists.

perro: dog; claro: of course ; Mi cuento es doloroso: My story is sad; Ven rápido: Come quickly; piloncillo: sugar cone ; Por el amor de Dios: For the love of God

Enrique Esparza (1828–1917), Alamo witness

Alamo Boy

Some say I made up a child's story, that mi cabeza vieja fills with imaginings. Pero, mi mente was always sharp. Still is. Dios es mi testigo, my pounding heart Papá's proud witness. Fui un niño de ocho años, in the heart of it, remember it well! Papá belonged to Benavides company of the American army. He moved our familia to the Alamo to join other Tejanos, Americanos, y hombres de todas partes. Pero, mi tío Francisco was on General Santa Anna's side. Fíjate nomás, dos hermanos, now a double-edged navaja.

Santa Anna's soldiers cut off the water. Only one well for our thirst. Their shifting bugle calls terrified us. Soon, guns and cannons thundered nonstop. Curdling death cries pierced the air in many languages. Papá Gregorio braved his cannon. I really wished for a weapon. Far outnumbered, the Alamo defenders kept up una fuerte pared. No turning back, they'd crossed the line on the ground.

I watched el cielo fill with rage. Both men and women died — even children. The siege continued for days. During a three-day armistice, Mamá was asked to flee with us. She told Papá, *if you're going to stay, so am I. If they kill one, they can kill us all.* También, me acuerdo de Travis, Bowie, y Crockett. The Mexicans called Crockett *Don Benito*, a tall, slim man, always at the head, ayudando, raising our spirits. Bowie, brave but too sick, weak, to fight; confined to a cot in a small room. Travis commanded the fort.

After many more days of batalla, we heard El Deguello, no quarter, from the Mexican side — Mejico's sangre beating through their and our venas: like their angry drums. Our promised reinforcements never arrived. In the end, they attacked like diablos in the dark. Women and children hid in a large quarter. Bullets whizzed closer to where I crouched with Mamá y mis hermanos, her face filled with fiery fear. A boy wrapped in a blanket was killed. Their soldados clambered up escaleras, swamped the fort. Both sides became wild animals in the dark. So close we heard swords clanging, escopetas exploding, bayonet blades plunging. When Papá's thumping cannon stopped, I knew his heart had too. Things got crazier, louder, endless.

When all the rumbling ceased, I saw pilas of lifeless cuerpos in a carnage of pooled blood. Shades of crimson plastered the walls. At daylight, the Mexicans began to remove the dead — this took several days. My father's brother convinced Santa Anna to give Papá a proper burial in the Campo Santo. Burned in mountainous pyres, all the Alamo corpses, including Travis, Crockett, and Bowie blazed for days, forming one ash. We were spared. Santa Anna demanded testimonio of events from Mamá and the others, gave each a blanket and two silver dollars, then set us free. He was later captured at San Jacinto, y la guerra se terminó. Un momento we were Mejicanos, the next we became Tejanos.

Anjela Villarreal Ratliff

At the age of eight, Enrique Esparza witnessed the Battle of the Alamo with his family. In his 70s and 80s, Mr. Esparza was interviewed by San Antonio newspapers. This sharp, bilingual, Tejano's account — almost excluded from history — sheds new light on the Alamo events.

mi cabeza vieja: my aged head; Pero, mi mente: But, my mind; Dios es mi testigo: God is my witness; Fui un niño de ocho años: I was a boy of eight years; y hombres de todas partes: and men from all parts; Pero, mi tío: But, my uncle; Fíjate nomás, dos hermanos: Just imagine, two brothers; navaja: knife; una fuerte pared: a strong wall; el cielo: the sky; Tambien, me acuerdo de: I also remember; ayudando: helping; batalla: battle; El Deguello: "no quarter,"; venas: veins; escaleras: ladders; escopetas: muskets; pilas: piles; cuerpos: bodies; Campo Santo: Sacred Cemetery; y la guerra se terminó: and the war ended; Un momento: One moment

Soldaderas (1835–1836)

After the Battles, What Will Become of Us?

Our legs will remember the march
  the creaking knees
  the scrape of boot over rock
  searching for a hold
  a level space on uneven ground.

So much of the battle is walking
  leaving our querido pueblo
  for this hostile terrain.

Hunger comes alive in us
  each pass of the bowl
  less to go around,
  the shedding of objects that defined us
  left behind on the road.

What is our inheritance
  when our soldados are gone,
  in this land
  claimed by the Anglos,
  who are newcomers here?
  They
  throw glances at our skin
  the black of our braids
  and wish that we would disappear.

We reclaim the fertility
  of mexicanidad,
  the will to form a new life
  in this República de Tejas.

Call it what you will.
We still call it our own.

    Leticia A. Urieta

During the Texas war with Mexico, Mexican women, known as Soldaderas, would accompany their husbands, fathers and brothers on the march and sometimes even into battle to help keep their men alive. This poem is written from one of those nameless women whose stories are often forgotten in mainstream historical accounts.

soldaderas: camp followers; querido: dear; soldados: soldiers

Susan Shelby Magoffin (1827–1855), diarist

The Roundness of Things

Susan Shelby Magoffin at Bent's Fort, 1846

Some said we'd been forty days upon the trail
before we'd reached that oven of a place.
At night I wrapped my body 'round the hope
within my belly, feared to feel its life blood drain away.

The first night there, the men had been, like me, tired,
sun-stunned, thirsting, unable to take food.
They'd fallen anywhere to have a bit of rest.
By the next night they were up and at their games,
with the slap of cards in the room next to mine
and the click of billiard balls. The wagon train went
on without us. I lay in the stifling room
the fort medico turned over for my care,
with wrung-out cloths pressed against my head,
flies buzzing round the doily on the chamber pot
that, all too soon, I would need to rise and use.
Although I prayed for my release, I could not
seem to leave off cramping even for an hour.

Then came the black night the others arrived.
All the noise from along the corridor
shifted to the storehouse underneath my room.
   — Wilder men with more and vicious games — I knew
what they were up to. The day we had arrived
I'd seen the clay circle stamped in the mud floor
beneath the drying fox furs stretched on hoops,
shelves of Native blankets, boxes of trade silver.
The pit was as perfect as the round rose window
in the apse of the cathedral where I'd wed
a year before, the cultured man who'd brought me here.

Now up rang the clink of coins, the eager shouts.
Beside myself, I left the sodden mattress,
to put my eye against the crooked floor and,
'twixt vigas and latillas, I spied an awful sight:
below, dusty men, unshaven, red with drink,
my husband there among them. He found me near dawn,
bleeding, on the floor. I'd finally lost the child.
The kitchen women fetched water from the well.
They bathed me; then they scrubbed the boards. My baby?
Wrapped in my best dress, interred outside the fort,
on the prairie, beneath stones meant to keep
the varmints out — too near the holes the men had dug
to bury roosters killed in the bloody ring.

I learned repugnant things in that far country.
I know folk can choose to use their artistry
to make round windows that open up the soul,
or pits, as round, that satisfy their lusting.
But, I am sure, the bright ring of God's sight is on us,
unblinking as the eye of the winning cock
that, next day, was stuffed feet-first into a saddle bag,
quick head jerking, and carried by a pony,
out into the countryside, on along the trail.

    Christine H. Boldt

This poem was inspired by the bare facts that young bride Susan Shelby Magoffin traveled west with her husband on the Santa Fe Trail in 1846 and suffered a miscarriage at Bent's Fort, CO. For Susan's own account of her journey, read Down the Santa Fe Trail and Into Mexico: The Diary of Susan Shelby Magoffin, 1846–1847.

vigas: beams; latillas: wood sticks laid across beams to form a celing

Pecos Bill (circa 1830), tall tale cowboy

Pecos Bill Reveals tha Truth

Not all tha tales folks tell are true.
Yep, I were raised by a mama coyote.
I had fleas an' howled at tha moon, but
like ma brother tole me: *Folks in Texas*
jus' do that. That ain't tha tale
I'm here ta tell ya.

I invented tha brandin' iron, lassoo,
an' cowboy ballad. I invented tarantulas
an' scorpions too, but I were jokin' then.
An' I rid a ole mountain lion so hard
tha air filled with fur, an' jackrabbits,
thinkin' it were night, went right off ta bed.
But none a that's matterin' taday.

Onct I rid a tornado clean 'cross Texas,
a-squeezin' rain outta it all tha way,
breakin' tha worse dang drought
we done had in years. Tied them rivers
in knots, flattened a few forests, renamed one
Staked Plains. But that ain't what I'm here
ta tell ya neither. I'm here ta tell ya
'bout ma wild, red-headed woman.

Firs' I laid eyes on Slue-Foot Sue
she were ridin' a giant catfish
down tha Rio Grande, reins in one hand
an' six-shooter in t'other a-plinkin' at clouds,
makin' right purty designs, too.
It were love at firs' sight, an' after
a few days courtin', I ast her ta marry me.

Well sir, no sooner had we said *I do*,
than Sue wanted ta ride ma horse,
Widder-Maker. She had on a purty white dress,
one a them stylish bustles — heavy-duty
steel springs from Sears & Roebuck —
on tha back. A course Widder-Maker
bucked her; she were bouncin' higher an' higher,
a wavin' an' a cryin' an' a throwin' kisses.
After five days I knowed she were gonna starve.

This here's where tha story gets kinda murky.
Some say she bumped her head on tha moon,
an' it kilt her. Some say I shot her, but
I coulda never did that. Or I lassooed her,
but she kept on a-bouncin' till we both
done landed on the moon. But that ain't true
'cause here I am.

A few say I lassood her, but she were so mad
she never spoke ta me agin. An' that's close.
Sue decided I were jus' too wild a critter
ta make a good husband. She shook ma hand
an' went back ta ridin' catfish; I went back
ta ma coyote pack. Y'all can hear me,
mos' ever' night, a-howlin'' an'
a-moanin' ma lost love.

   Ann Howells

Pecos Bill is a Southwest legend who embodies all the ideals of the cowboy in much the same way that Paul Bunyan embodies the ideals of the Northwest lumberjack. Larger than life, Bill is the roughest toughest cowboy of them all. He invented the lasso, branding iron, cowboy ballad, and the rodeo. Tales of his exploits are plentiful and often have many different versions. Bill is known, not just in Texas, but all across the Southwest.

Slue-Foot Sue (circa 1830), tall tale daredevil

Slue-Foot Sue to Pecos Bill

All the things you've done to prove your love!
You've snuffed out all the fires in the sky
and in your heart to let one burn the brightest
in the indigo of night. You've lassoed
spring to make a sweet bouquet for me,
bluebonnets, marigolds and prickly pear.
You've got down on one knee with just a promise,
offered me the diamond of your eye.

But none of this, dear Bill, is good enough.
If you love me, let me be your equal,
ride at your side, not clinging to your waist.
Step off that high horse, let me in your saddle —
show me that you're man enough to love
a woman with a will as strong as yours.

Katherine Hoerth

Slue-Foot Sue is a fictional girlfriend of Pecos Bill. In the tall tales, we only learn about her through her experiences with Bill, but here is a poetic imagining of what she might have to say to the legend himself.

Territories to Statehood (1849–1918)

Vigilance

I was the first to rise
outside of Eden's gate,
thick, fleshly leaves unbending
in the dry, mourning wind,
thriving on thirst and rock
and shallow soil,
tightly holding back
buds that
open only briefly to worship
an infrequent rain;

piercing thorns draw blood
from man and beast alike
who risk impalement,
existing comfortably
in desolation
and testifying of a Creator
relentless in His
calling forth of
man's vigilance,
strength and blood —

the price to be paid
for survival
outside of Eden's gate.

Sally Clark

In the difficult landscape of the American desert Southwest, cactus grow naturally without care or maintenance. For generations, cactus have been planted as natural fences, forming a boundary line to keeps humans and animals out as well as in. Constant vigilance is required to prevent them from spreading as even when they are chopped down, they will often grow back.

Two mules (circa 1852), from a Cather novel

The Road to Mora: A Tanka Tale

Prelude: Following the United States' annexation of the New Mexico Territory in 1848, two former school friends, Father Latour and Father Valiant, are sent to reinvigorate the Catholic Church after nearly three hundred years of neglect under Spanish and Mexican rule. Father Valiant, now Vicar to Archbishop Latour, is returning to Santa Fe from an errand of mercy in Albuquerque. He stops one night at the rancho of a rich Mexican, Manuel Lujon, and, in the morning, with the cunning of a man who knows how to get his way gently, wheedles the gift of two cream-colored mules, Contento and Angelica — Contento for him and Angelica for his compadre, Father Latour.

a small wiry man
springs onto my back
with the agility of a grasshopper
shaking myself, I bolt
but then accept my load

The Divine of Man and Beast mates me with a holy man — he must have been so, for though he is ugly to other men and has a wart on his chin, even strangers feel love for him as soon as they meet. Angelica's man also is holy, but in a more refined way. If not love, respect is his grace. We head out on a mission to the village of Mora.

we clomp through rain
our coats matted and tufted
by icy winds
ahead the man sits straight
my man is low in the saddle

The rain drives at a slant through the air, with raindrops the size of tadpoles. I am tired and hungry. Rain turns to sleet and then hailstones bounce off my back. Upfront, Angelica's head is dropped low. Her rider turns and calls back to us that perhaps it is time to stop here, as daylight is beginning to fail. Angelica's head raises and then drops again as my rider responds, "Push on. We will come to shelter of some kind before the night sets in."

are we born this way?
they say a mule is stubborn
a man of faith
would say he is steadfast —
my doubt is broad and deep

Before the hour is up, indeed we approach an adobe house on the edge of a steep ravine. It is a poor and mean looking place. A man comes out the front door and speaks language I have never heard. This is my first American. We are put in the stable and fed grain. But Angelica and I are not at rest. Uneasy, we feel trepidation. We thank the Divine that we have not been unsaddled, for suddenly our two men burst into the stable. We need no urging. Off we go.

night closes
rain as heavy as ever
I feel the trust
as my man accepts my lead
Angelica and I find Mora

    Neal Whitman

In her iconic novel of the American Southwest, Death Comes for the Archbishop, *Willa Cather transforms two historic persons, Archbishop Jean-Baptiste Lamy and Vicar Joseph Machebeuf, into the fictional Father Jean Marie Latour and Father Joseph Valiant. Rather than give one of those historic or fictional personae voices in my poem, I chose one of the two mules who carried them across the New Mexcio territory in their travels across this vast landscape. Amelia Fielden, a proponent of the tanka tale explains that these are meant to "combine prose and tanka poems in a coherent, meaningful, and hopefully lyrical way."*

Emily D. West/Yellow Rose of Texas (circa 1815–1891), folk heroine

I Am Rose

This is what you'll find if you unzip history,
music pulsing in the cage of my ribs.
In the dark pipe of his longing,
my man makes a song for me.
White notes burst in his belly
when he thinks about the full nectar of my lips.

He keeps my name in the pocket of his tongue,
calls me his *yellow girl*.
Anonymity doesn't keep me safe
from the long arms of lust.
My beauty is a magnet.

He sings of diamonds and dew;
the hard light of my eyes is a hammer
drumming against hungry hands
reaching to lift the skirt of my womanhood.

Heat climbs down the ladder of morning
three rungs at a time, descends on the day
with a heavy foot; he tells me he's leaving.
I listen to his reasons, promises of return.
My face waters with sweat, tears, knowing
I will not take him back into the folds of my love.

This quiet dusk I watch the sky float in the Rio Grande,
dream of the waves of muscles swelling
across his broad back, the camber of his mouth,
hard handsome face softening when he backs
away from me. I remember our fingers sliding
off the cliff of our grasp, the cavern of emptiness.

I shudder; the next touch will not be his.
I feel the petals of my want withering
along the pebbled-stone of distance.

Loretta Diane Walker

"The plaintive courtship-themed 1853 lyrics of 'The Yellow Rose of Texas' fit the minstrel genre by depicting an African-American singer, who is longing to return to "a yellow girl," a term used to describe a mulatto, or mixed-race female born of African-American and white progenitors. *This iconic song of modern Texas and a popular traditional American tune, has experienced several transformations of its lyrics and periodic revivals in popularity since its appearance in the 1850s."* ~ The Handbook of the Texas Historical Association

Silvia King (circa 1813–1937), slave

Years Following Her Death, Former Texas Slave Silvia King Speaks to a Kidnapped Nigerian Girl

I tell you, my daughter, ideas are dangerous,
especially the thought of a self —

imagining you can name who you really are, choose
where you will stand in this world.

That is why they took you, herded you from school:
you had entered ideas as if they were oceans

and you the navigator riding the waves.	I know.
More than a century ago, I too was taken, not from a schoolyard

but from fields that fed my family — husband and children — taken
as if the life I was making was just dew upon the grass.

The ocean I crossed was a writhing beneath my back,
and the unclean smells of those shackled alongside me.

I too was stripped, presented at market, told where to stand
in a language that sounded like the tearing apart of trees,

a language I use to speak now.	I learned
to inhabit my body by frequenting places where no one would look —

secret folds within my soul where I felt the faces of my children,
heard their voices pronounce my true name. You must make it

enough: if not the dream you once harbored of being a doctor,
then the motion of ideas rooted already in you.

When men you do not choose make you feel skinless,
there is still the idea of outliving their ignorance, idea of

unexpected kindness rising beside you, a butterfly from the thistles.
Here is my voice — still alive and testifying across the ages —

it recognizes you, and holds, holds you in prayer.
There is so much more than any of us can see.

Cyra S. Dumitru

Silvia King was a free African woman turned Texas slave, who lived long enough to experience emancipation in the United States. According to her oral narrative reproduced in Texas Tears and Texas Sunshine, Voices of Frontier Women, *edited by Jo Ella Powell Exley, Silvia was kidnapped in Africa as a married mother and sold on the auction block to a white man who brought her to live in Marlin, Texas. Her story was recorded as part of the Federal Writers' Project of the Works Project Administration charged with the specific purpose of interviewing former slaves.*

Cochise (circa 1804–1874), Apache leader

Cut the Tent

Thomas,
my brother-in-truth,
bury me in the sun-struck crevice
I showed you once
in Dragoon Mountains,
but don't reveal my tomb.
Bury me with black, vermillion
and yellow war marks
on my oak-bark skin,
but remind them that nobody
craved peace more than I did.

I signed this treaty,
yet my heart is not at peace.
I wanted my people to ride free,
straight as lances
where rocks & trees talk with us —
not to crouch like coyotes
cornered in a corral.
I trust General Howard,
but others, whose word
is like paper, come soon
for our silver and copper.

Thomas, my struggle is over —
I'm tired of hanging on the side
of my horse's neck,
counterstrikes and retaliation
for their chicanery and deceit.
Bury me with a knife.
I cut the tent
to see my slain father

meeting me at Apache Pass,
a claw of hummingbird
attached to my new cradle.

Elina Petrova

"Nobody wants peace more than I do. Why shut me up on a reservation? We will make peace; we will keep it faithfully. But let us go around free as Americans do." These words of the Chiricahua Apache chief Cochise, quoted by his youngest son, Naiche, became the starting point for my poem. Leaders who devote their lives to fair play seldom if ever win, but I wish they were a less rare breed. Learning about Cochise, I was fascinated with the honesty, courage, strategic resourcefulness, and bitter diplomatic wisdom of this larger-than-life tragic figure in Native American history. The story of his friendship with Thomas Jeffords, a U.S. Army scout in the Arizona Territory, who became Cochise's blood brother, touched me immensely. Cochise's secret burial site in the Dragoon Mountains, known only by the Chiricahua Apache and Jeffords, became another source for my inspiration. The poem's title refers to the 1861 incident when, wrongly accused of raiding the ranch of John Ward, Cochise was lured into Lieutenant George Bascom's camp at Apache Pass and threatened to be kept as a hostage until Ward's property and step-son were returned. Infuriated by the humiliating, unjust imprisonment, Cochise sliced his way through Bascom's tent and slipped away from the guards who surrounded the tent. Sources: Sweeney, Edwin R., Cochise: Chiricahua Apache Chief; Lockwood, Frank C., The Apache Indians; Arnold, Elliott, Blood Brother.

Paula Angel (circa 1842–1861), murderer

Hanging Day for Paula Angel, April 1861

People came from all over New Mexico
to watch me hang.
Claire who gave me apples in the fall,
Marlin and Elena who had known me
since we chased grasshoppers
in the dirt as children.
Half of the crowd must have known me.
The gamblers and saloon keepers
and the soldiers came too.
It must be a strange thing to stand
with your neighbors and watch
another human strangled by a rope
just before you must put the beans
on the fire for dinner.

They say I murdered my lover.
My sister says he was a lying bastard.
In jail, I was knees to the ground,
trying to face God, while each morning
Sherriff Herrera counted down the days to me
like a death clock. He picked the tallest
cottonwood in the county to hang me from,
drove me to it on a bright April morning
in a wagon with my own coffin.

Blank faces met us at the tree, but at the start
of the hanging, the sheriff forgot to tie my hands,
pulled the wagon away,
and I climbed up the rope,
rescued myself from the arms of death.

The crowd helped me down,
ready to free me and surrender to what was.
People said I had been hanged,

that was enough.
But the sheriff looked mad
and some colonel stepped up,
saying the order must be carried out
to death.
There is always one heckler.

And once more the wagon.
Once more the rope
and then a quick intake of breath,
and then . . .
I imagine the offspring of those I knew
still talk about betrayal
and some thin line between love and death.
I see their faces in the crowd,
bright lovely faces.
I imagine their children on warm spring days
chase grasshoppers that jump in the dirt.

. . . I never closed my eyes.

Liza Wolff-Francis

The speaker is Paula Angel, who, for many years, was said to have been the only woman to have ever been hanged in New Mexico.

Cynthia Ann Parker/Naduah (1825–1871), Comanche captive

Nadua's Prayer

Hear me, Great Spirit, my Prairie Flower burns
with fever, the last of my family
left to me, torn from my sons, my husband's body
beneath the cloudless sky, blue as
the eyes that betrayed me to my captors.

Hear me, Great Spirit, when I was taken
from father and mother, I came to live
with my people, who wanted me as their own
daughter, She Who Is Found, no longer
Cynthia Ann, no longer the white man's.

Hear me, Great Spirit, I have given birth
to warriors, horsemen of the Comanche,
Quanah and Pecos of the red canyons
who were but little boys orphaned
when Rangers killed Peta and kidnapped me.

Hear me, Great Spirit, I will be buried
in exile far from the tribe of my heart
by familiar strangers, for I'll have left
no hunger for meat, no thirst for water
no spirit to breathe, if this child should die.

Katherine Durham Oldmixon

Nadua's (Cynthia Ann Parker's) is perhaps the most famous of Native American captive stories. She was taken in a Comanche raid on Fort Parker in central Texas when she was about nine years old, and by all accounts had completely assimilated into the Comanche community when Texas Rangers raided and killed her husband Peta and separated her from her sons Quanah and Pecos. She was taken with her infant daughter, Topsannah (Prairie Flower), who died of pneumonia. Nadua died shortly afterward, having refused to eat.

Calamity Jane/Martha Jane Canary (1852–1903), frontierswoman

How to Be a Woman in a Hostile World

This world will spit you out like spent tobacco
if you let it. Gals like us, the poor,
were made to spend our lives down on our knees,
barefoot, our tongues a useless piece of flesh.

But child, you have my blood within your veins,
which means you won't be satisfied with life
unless you spend it like a tumbleweed
in the wind, no roots to hold you down.
To find yourself you have to learn to break

the porcelain of your skin, the rules, your heart —
cook breakfast for a lover as you smoke
a fat cigar, wear rugged cowboy boots
beneath your petticoats so you can lift
your dress and run if danger strikes (it will),
sing lullabies to orphans, air your lungs
out cussing by the campfire with the drunks,
tend the sick and dying with your left
hand on the pearly pistol at your hip.

Lean on nothing but your own broad shoulders,
be hero and be damsel of your tale.
The real calamity is wasting life
in the dust of someone else's wagon.
Trust your gut to lead you out of Dodge,
and may your greatest sin be wanderlust.

Katherine Hoerth

This poem is written in the voice of Calamity Jane and is addressed to her daughter. Legend has it that she wrote a series of letters to a daughter she gave up for adoption as an infant.

Kitty Leroy (1850–1878), gambler

Kitty Leroy Proposes Marriage

Let me shoot an apple off your head;
it's the only way to prove you're right
for me, the only way that we can wed.

You know my reputation, what's been said
about the way I handle guns, my tight
grip. I can shoot an apple off your head

with both eyes closed, half-drunk, in heels instead
of boots. So let me have a go tonight —
if you survive, my darling, we'll be wed.

The chamber's belly's loaded up with lead —
now all you have to say is yes, to bite
the bullet with my gun aimed at your head

to prove your love and trust in me. I said
that I don't need a man who's rich or bright —
I need a man with balls of steel to wed

a crazy gal like me. I aim, I spread
my legs, I close my eyes and dream of night.
Just let me shoot that apple off your head —
if you survive, my darling, we'll be wed.

Katherine Hoerth

According to legend, Kitty Leroy used to shoot apples off the head of her first husband. Here is a poetic reimagining of how she convinced him to let her try the first time.

Kitty Leroy (1850–1878), gambler

Trigger Kiss

No one knows more about softness
than the woman with a switchblade in her garter.
My gypsy jingle gives you a heart murmur.
You crave to tame, rub against my glittering.
Just wake me up when your gun is loaded with luck.
All of the gentlemen are dying to be shot.

They'd rather risk blood than to love.
A woman is supposed to be filled
with the echoing giggle of babies.
A woman can't be left alone, but I unbutton
your lies, I decipher your deck of lullabies.
No one knows more about love

than the woman pouring the whiskey.
I fold up dollar bills into roses for the girls.
I am the bullet in my gun, my kiss is my trigger.
Everyone knows what I do on my back.
I grant my own wishes, flipping tails
to heads. I suffer no language of loss.

Amanda Chiado

Kitty Leroy was an infamous independent woman, gunslinger, prostitute, and gambler of the Old West.

Antonio José Martínez (1793–1867), priest, educator, leader

Padre Martínez Goes To Heaven

Hola, Frenchman, es una sorpresa to find *me* here, qué no?

Excommunicating me didn't work in spite of your fine statue, the one of you standing as straight and slim as an aspen sapling, looking down your aquiline nose.

You, Frenchman, you gave the poor a cathedral when all they needed were iglesias built of mud bricks. To call the people to mass, you gave them a bell. I, their bell-shaped padre, laughed when I saw it. And what of los Penitentes, those holy men who kept the faith alive when Rome ignored us? They inflicted pain on themselves, taking on our sins as our Lord did, but in return for their sacrifices you tried to dishonor them, to keep them from their sacred rites. "Un necio is pleased with his own folly," my mother used to say.

You came to our land, head held high, cold fire in your heart. You rattled on like a magpie about tithes. "Blessed are the poor," you said. What about your vow of poverty, you who lived in a large house and wore fine robes? If tithes meant so much to you, why didn't you sell what you had and pay them?

Ay Dios, Dios, why did you let the Holy Father send an uppity Frenchman to la tierra de mi querencia, my Penitente land where I built schools for my people and for los Indios too? I even built a printing press. Casa Martínez became la iglesia for my flock so they could come to pray when they had nowhere else to go. "*Vamos a la casa de Dios*," they said when they came.

Forgive me, Dios, but la gente de la tierra de mi corazón meant nothing to him. Like a patrón, he demanded tithes, then when the people couldn't pay, he took away the sacraments. What kind of priest would do that?

Sharon Rhutasel-Jones

Educator, politician, publisher and priest, José Antonio Martínez championed the poor and made the sacraments available before the Catholic Church officially entered New Mexico. After the Church sent Archbishop Jean-Baptiste Lamy to establish the archdiocese of Santa Fe, Martínez refused to collect tithes as per Lamy's orders. As a result, the Archbishop ordered Padre Martínez's excommunication. A beloved figure among his people, Padre Martínez became a nineteenth-century folk hero in northern New Mexico.

una sorpresa: a surprise; iglesias: churches; un necio: fool; la tierra de mi querencia: the land of my affection; la gente: people; corazón: heart

Hanged man (circa 1880s)

Nameless Man

You grew up on a farm west of Selma
because your great-grandfather rode
his horse seven miles west, to Laton
where on that village's main street
I hung by the neck, the rope's noose
looped over branch of a valley oak.
So your ancestor turned around and
galloped back east that little way to
buy 120 acres from Leland Stanford's
crooked railroad. Did I steal a horse or
money from a till? What was my crime,
if any, what court and jury sentenced
me to die? The oak still grows there
but the rope is gone. What was my name,
my wife's, children's, mother's? Where
was I from and where is my grave?
Cyrus Davis never knew or stopped
to ask a reason. My nameless body
pointed the direction to where your
better life was lived — where you grew
and worked the land, dug furrows, pruned
plums and grapevines, drank cold pump
water straight from underground, fished
tulle pond for glinting bluegill, rowed
green boat under close early stars, saw
Venus and made a wish, found a horse's
tooth, ghostly Belgians' giant shoes in
sand. I told your mother's father's father
to find his truer place, dry leaves rustling,
worn boots swinging in a morning wind.

Nels Hanson

The nameless man is nameless but alive in memory, his destiny intertwined with five generations of my family.

Belle Starr/Myra Maybelle Shirley Reed Starr (1848–1889), outlaw

Belle Starr's Last Lament

Perhaps you won't judge me
too harshly, just because I have a fondness
for feathered hats, velvet riding clothes and men
with dusky-colored skin. Yes, it might be true
some of them were horse thieves. Maybe
I was too. Or maybe you're just jealous
because I looked good in the saddle, riding high
through the hills I adopted when I married
two Cherokees — Sam, and, later, his younger cousin,
Jim, who I admit I only took up with in order to keep
living on land I never had a right to anyway ... but then,
is that reason enough to malign me? Or is it just
that you wish you could spend your last night dancing,
drinking and carrying on, the belle of the ball,
never suspecting you'd be shot in the back in the dark
as you led your horse to water, bending close
to hear him whinny with contentment
as the stream circled 'round you, and the sky
opened to wrap you in a blanket of stars.

Margaret Dornaus

Belle Starr, known as the "Queen of the Oklahoma Bandits," crossed paths with many Western outlaws, including the James and Younger gangs, before settling down in Oklahoma Territory to a life of horse thievery with Sam Starr. Her 1889 murder remains a mystery.

E.B. Salsig (circa 1864–circa 1921), lumber manager

Death Smells like Cinnamon

In the carnival tintype you looked like a promise.
The painted background ... I memorized the lines,
each like a twilight desert path to water.

I told you I would keep it forever. I even thought
I might. But that afternoon ... imagine! ...
there was the crack

(small, really) and then the sun became a candle
slim, wavering, and its center:
the bright fiery kiss of a cigar tip to skin.

I believe I lay there a long time.
I imagined the scent of death: hot, sweet, woody —
like cinnamon. You must think I am mad.

Everywhere here are men buried inside rocks
and in the spaces between the grains of sand:
the Mexican woodcutters shot last week by Geronimo's men

and the horsethieves we hanged and hanged and hanged again
from the windmill derrick until
the water went foul. We mine ore

from their bones every day. And I know
one day my name will be lost among theirs.
Yet, at that moment, all I could picture

were the words that were gone, your words lost behind
that hole, vanished forever in a great silent ellipsis.
Only then did I really want to kill him, to dash him wetly on stones.

In the shadow and dirt, as the men gathered round,
wheezing dust and blood, I reached up,
touched the bullet in my breast

pocket. And it came to me: perhaps they were not really lost —
maybe they were forced clean through,
your script now written in me.

Perhaps the letters now swirled within:
the flourished *E*'s inside my lungs,
stray legs of perfumed *R*'s rising in my blood.

Women gasped when I took the parcel from my pocket,
blood soaked like a holy thing. And from the road I rose,
smiled, looked about for a fast horse.

J. Todd Hawkins

In November 1882, in Total Wreck, Arizona, a disagreement broke out between businessman E.B. Salsig and John Drummond over the sale of a mine. Drummond called Salsig into the street to resolve the quarrel. Once outside, Salsig punched Drummond, who then drew on and shot Salsig. One bullet struck him in the chest, but was stopped by a wallet filled with a thick bundle of love letters that Salsig was carrying, saving his life.

W. A. White (1847–1916), photographer

About My Photography

Raton, New Mexico, 1880s

The desert's dressed like saloon gals —
orange, yellow, purple, gray, green, brown, red.
My albumen prints don't do right by the colors.
W. A., I say to myself, *someday
they'll patent a way to fix that.*

Towering white clouds in the bluest skies —
folks back East can't stretch
their lungs to drink in this clear air,
can't step back to take in
the outcroppings and cliffs.
The cowboys at the bunk house
posing with horses, dogs,
a novelty to swells in
Philadelphia and Boston.

I can't capture the flies, mosquitoes,
the stink of men, animals,
the rushing sound of creeks.
The dog on the tracks surely feels
the rumble of the approaching train.
Fantastical idea, sound with pictures.
When the healer Francis Schlatter
blew through town, his stare
bore a hole through me;
that's something my lens did catch.

A log ranch house hugs a hillside;
a brick home, grander, with bee hives.
I 'bout froze my butt off at that mine one winter.

But I like the hiking, the trips to Colorado, the peace.
I live day by day, don't worry
if I'm famous as Mathew Brady.

Sylvia Riojas Vaughn

The speaker in this poem is little-known photographer W. A. White (1847–1916), who opened a studio in Raton, New Mexico, in 1881, capturing people and events in the town, as well as surrounding landscapes, ranches, mines and railroads. His work is available online through the Ohio Wesleyan University Photographs of the American Southwest (1870s–Early 1900s) Digital Collections.

Loretto Chapel staircase (1877/1881–present)

Loretto Chapel, Santa Fe, New Mexico

The Sisters of the Chapel
made a novena to St. Joseph,
patron saint of carpenters.
On the ninth and final day of prayer
a man with a donkey and a toolbox
appeared, looking for work.
"I will build the staircase you need to the choir loft,"
he said. "However, I must work in total privacy."

As he crafted me —
a beautiful, spiral staircase
with no visible means of support —
he prayed and sang hymns of praise.
Each slab of wood smiled
as I, the beautiful staircase, progressed.
Those smiles remain in the grain.

My elegant circular structure complete,
the carpenter left
never to be seen or heard from again.

Many experts have tried to decipher my mystery
but have failed.

I know the secret but I will not tell.

    Von S. Bourland

To this day, no one knows the identity of the carpenter, nor how he constructed the staircase using no nails.

Eugene F. Rogers (1854–1941), merchant

Silky Rogers

I didn't come from Tennessee or Kentucky,
with a corn-bread making wife. I came from
St. Johnsberry, Vermont with a college-educated
wife. I left the icy sheets of nor'easters. I took stage-
coaches, clipper ships, carried newspapers bought
for a nickel in Sacramento, tin plates to pan for gold,
iron picks to coax silver from mountain-rock to sell
to the dream-addicted lonely bachelors who stole
from the earth, mountain rivers to capture their fortunes.
I made 8% profit on the soaps, shirts, and coffee, more
on newspapers. From the Klondike Pass, Sitka, Everett,
Anacortes, Sacramento, Ventura, Santa Barbara,
San Bernardino, Prescott, Bisbee, Nogales, and Tombstone
I built 35 stores. I became the Father Serra of dry-goods.
I bought a silk hat in San Francisco and they called me Silky.
I wore a beaver coat I bought from a trapper in Alaska.
I never drank whiskey. I won poker games. I crouched
under the table at Tombstone when the cow thieves Ike
and Billy Clanton and Frank and Tom McLaury shot
their pistols at the O.K. Corral. The Earp brothers and
Doc Holiday gained the fame, I buried my suffragette-
marching wife, kept brothers, cousins on the payroll, tithed
and died in my sleep at 92. Now, tell me who won the West?

Joan Canby

Eugene F. Rogers left St. Johnsberry, Vermont, in the 1880s. He won enough money in a poker game on a ferry on the Erie Canal to purchase a ticket to go around the Horn to California. He landed in Santa Barbara, California, when it was still on the gold standard. He built a mercantile career by supplying dry goods, food, clothing, furniture to the early settlers from Alaska to Nogales, Arizona. Eugene Rogers was a fascinating man, never drank, sold his Arizona stores to the Goldwater family, left the Congregationalist church during WWI to become a Presbyterian because the pacifist pastor burnt the American flag . . . he was very American — and the great-grandfather of the author.

Old Joe (circa 1870s–circa 1900s), horse

Old Joe

Tonight could nearly be the other frosted nights
we traveled together, the doctor and I, our road
winding between winter fields, a cold fog
soft and pale as goose down drifting in the gullies.
The buckboard's wheels and leather harness creaking,
its oil lamps swaying yellow on their hooks.
My iron-shod hooves striking light from flint shards
in my path, so that any creature alert in tree or burrow
could spy us coming, lit by licks of igneous flame,
by my haunches lamp-slicked, glistening.
After we called upon his patients I would take him home —
and home, and home — as he drowsed, dog-tired,
blanketed in wool, certain I would always know our way.

From restless dreams he sometimes muttered the name
he gave me, *Joe*, his sleep raw as the stars burning
in the tar above our heads, helpless in their pain of endings,
beginnings. He ought well have been accustomed
to such pains, having pulled half the county headfirst
into this world, slipped the other half into the next.
When he woke I sensed his gentling hands, the flick
of ghostly reins, as I paced forever forward.

More than twenty useful years I gave him,
drawing his buckboard over ruts and stones, across
blistered prairie, through spring pastures thorny
with mesquite, ofttimes past this dusty cotton field
where I now lie in a pen built of white pickets straight
as the traces that once lay on my flanks, straight
as duty. I rest in the earth on one side, no better
than a failed crop ploughed under. I would stand,
but lack a harness, a wagon hitched behind.

And cold has fallen on the land again, a cold more
withering than I recollect, bone-deep, sharp as the smell
of mountain juniper in the circlet of green needles
someone places at my head each winter.

It was cold the evening of our final journey.
I had stood hours in a patient's barren acre,
blowing steam, stamping to stay warm, waiting
for the doctor to bow out the door after staying late
to share the family's supper. When I saw him tip his hat
goodbye to them and step down from the porch
I started forward with the wagon. How then
could I leave him? I have always pulled his burdens,
his needs. He counts on me. I must rise somehow
from this hard ground, see him safely home.

Susan Rooke

Old Joe was the horse of Dr. W.W. Fowler, a country doctor who practiced in Runnels County, Texas, in the late 1800s. Night and day, fair weather and foul, the doctor traveled to attend to his far-flung patients in a buckboard wagon pulled by Joe. When Joe died at 31 after many years of service, the doctor buried his beloved horse on his farm south of Ballinger, in a white picket-fenced enclosure that can still be seen from U.S. Highway 83. It's wonderful and touching that the enclosure is still kept up nicely and decorated with a new wreath each December, more than 100 years after Joe died.

Teresa Urrea (1873–1906), folk healer

The Healer, Santa Teresa Urrea

Santa, they call me saint.

Ask where the power comes from,
Where does it reside.

The power rises up
Pushing against my impatient fingers
One touch and then
I renew them
For life is renovable
Circuitous as the blood
Rushing in the veins
The tendons knitting back together
The miracle done.

The poder lived in me all along,
It is nothing new
For we are a People of renewal
Of transplantation
Of Revolution
Eternidad, like the rebozo
Interwoven in our rebirth.

They call me Santa Teresa
The Healer of Cabora.
Peeled away, under many names
Curandera, heretic, india, immigrant, exile
Spectacle,
I have the power to ignite.
The People light candles
Which awaken my image,
And pray out my name

The ritual of eternity
That keeps me alive
In the smooth, resolute flame.

   Leticia A. Urieta

Teresa Urrea was an inspirational and controversial Tejana figure. The daughter of a Mayo ranch worker and the powerful ranch owner, she was trained early in the indigenous arts of healing, and later was declared a saint when she began to perform miracles of healing after a violent attack. She was exiled from Sonora, Mexico, to Arizona and later El Paso by the Porfiriato, but remained the inspiration for many indigenous Mexican uprisings against the government of Porfirio Diaz, and is still considered a highly influential Tejana and mestiza woman.

renovable: renewable; poder: power; rebozo: shawl; india: Indian

Teresa Urrea (1873–1906), folk healer

The Hopeless Christened Me the Saint of Cabora

Clifton, Arizona.

The air, good for consumption.
Yet I spit up blood
brilliant as sunsets of the Sonoran Desert,
scarlet as peaks at twilight in El Paso.

In those places, in countless others,
countless times I said,
Go. You are healed, thanks be to God.
Not a coin did I pocket.

They say I've used up my life force.
In my youth in Mexico, I traveled past golden wheat,
tumors no longer plaguing the farmer because of my touch.
I put mothers in their childbeds into trances to ease birth.
How grateful I felt when I helped the blind see,
when paralyzed limbs moved again —
free to weave, herd, perform the Dance of the Deer.

I, Teresa Urrea, a nobody, a woman,
yet in the year 1880 the Holy Mother
blessed me with the power to cure
as I slumbered for months; I rose
only when Father prepared me for burial.
And when I woke, I began to speak
with the Yaqui, the Mayo, the Tarahumara
of freedom from injustice as well as pain.
I said God wanted them to keep their lands.
President Díaz was wrong to drive them off.

But I was a match lighting the fuse of rebellion.
Government forces murdered
women and children in Tomochic.
Oh! My cries echoed against the red canyon walls.
My tears watered the prickly pear.
My prayers filled the limitless skies.

Soldiers exiled Father and me.
I traveled America, practicing
my ancient art of curanderismo.
Those I trusted lied, charging
the sick for my gift.
Men came and went, leaving me
two precious daughters.

Am I a heretic, as the Church says?
Or Heaven sent, as the people say?
I cough, feeling neither saint nor demon.

Sylvia Riojas Vaughn

The speaker in this poem is folk healer (curandera in Spanish) Teresa Urrea, originally of Mexico, whose family moved to Sonora, Mexico, in 1880 to escape political reprisals from dictator Porfirio Díaz. After falling into a cataleptic state for more than three months, she awoke with miraculous curing powers and a message to Mexican Indians that seizure of their lands by Díaz was wrong. Díaz sent troops to exile her to the United States when rebellion ensued, where she lived in El Paso and Arizona, denying in the press her role in the violence, and touring American cities to heal the sick (practicing folk healing, or curanderismo in Spanish), denounced by the Catholic Church.

Dolores Gavino Doporto (circa 1830–1893), widow and legend

Dolores

> *"It is only the crazy old Mexican woman with her fire."*
> ~ General B.H. Grierson, Fort Davis

¡O José, O Querido!
Weeping, I struggle to climb the trail
my desperate feet have worn
into these scrub brush hills.
La noche mocks my anguish:
above me, las estrellas shine like una fiesta.
In the canyon, the scattered fort lamps
of soldiers guard against what hides
in the night — they did not save you.

La luna pulls me up the rocky path,
her glowing face, a ghost
of your tender smile, your soft eyes
enticing me with desire.
Like coyote, I howl!
By candlelight women listen
with the ears of their hearts for my chillidos
and whisper, *Ella se ha vuelto loco.*

¡Ay Querido, ven acá!
Let me once again press my nose
into the flower of your scent,
my lips against your mouth,
my breasts to your músculos fuertes...

¿Eres tu, José? I feel you
in el cierzo — its breath moans
your devotion to our flame!
Watch as I kneel, bend, blow life
onto the coals of what I have left.

The tinder of my splintered heart ignites
the sky in fits of pain, my wails rise
like the embers of our love. . . .
¿O Querido, puede ver mi fuego?

    Anne McCrady

A Fort Davis legend holds that in the mid-1800s, a young Mexican woman named Dolores Gavino Doporto often lit a signal fire atop a mountain as a message to her fiancé, a goatherd out with his flock. When he was murdered by Mescalero Apaches shortly before their wedding day, locals claimed she lost her mind, lighting nighttime fires atop a hill for the rest of her life. The site was later named Dolores Mountain. Dolor is Spanish for "pain."

Querido: loved one; chillidos: screams; Ella se ha vuelto loco: She has gone mad; ven acá: come here; músculos fuertes: strong muscles; el cierzo: the north wind; puede ver mi fuego: can you see my fire

We'wha (1849–1896), Zuni Two-Spirit

Two-Fold, One-Kind

They don't know what to make of me,
don't have a word for *lhamana*.
Beyond my skirts and sashes,
my deliberate, short stride,
I, We'Wha, am the tallest of A:shiwi.
My shoulders, my hands,
my jaw are giveaways that
I am one of the elite of my pueblo.
But most whites choose
to see me as a woman, even
Tilly, who studies our people.

In 1885, she took me to Washington,
where I was celebrated as a princess,
a priestess, a Zuni maiden.
I attended teas, receptions, balls,
made calls like society women.
I bought a red-satin parasol
and carried it everywhere.
The National Museum, the Smithsonian,
even the White House welcomed me.
At the National Theatre,
I took part in the "Indian dance,"
waving my prayer stick
in time to their strange music
as I stood among their savage
bronzed and blackened faces,
whites pretending to be my kind.

I returned to the home of my auntie,
returned to my household duties,
made pottery like our women,
wove blankets like our men,

counseled like our lhamanas
have done for thousands of years.

But the white world crushes in,
withers us with guns and soldiers.
Now, imprisoned in Fort Wingate,
I am a captive of my gender.
Some mistake my quiet for ignorance.
But I have learned the language
of these white men, their words:
invert, man-woman, mujerado,
transvestite, freak, berdache.
Beyond these walls, another
jail, which they call a reservation.
Soon, no room for two-folds
or A:shiwi or the way of our gods:
assimilation, their word for eradication.

    Scott Wiggerman

We'wha was a Native American who was born male but lived her life as a female, a lhamana, a Zuni gender that combined both male and female elements (now called "Two-Spirit"). She was one of the few Zuni who learned English, which enabled her to became close friends with the anthropologist Matilda Coxe Stevenson, who did not realize We'wha's biological sex despite living with her for six months in Washington, D.C., where We'wha was treated as royalty, before returning to New Mexico, where she was arrested and imprisoned for insubordination. Upon her death, We'wha was buried in both pants and a dress. Source: Roscoe, Will, The Zuni Man-Woman.

lhamana: a mixed gender role; A:shiwi: Zuni

Henry Ossian Flipper (1856–1940), soldier

Dear John Letter on Behalf of My Dignity

After reading my Brief through, you will understand and appreciate the struggle I made to rise above the station to which I was born.

How does slavery smell?
Like everything
you do not want your children to hold.

I left the circumstances of my birth in Atlanta
to live with practitioners of prejudice at West Point.
Their moon-colored, ghost-colored, cotton-colored faces
were cities, cold citadels I avoided.
My skin was a wall they could not scale.

In the south, heat burned a black man's pride.
At the Point, ostracism was a weapon aimed at my ego.
Officers were not gentle men;
again and again they promoted
me to the rank of exclusion.
In class, I was crowded by inches of isolation.

At the Fort, my court martial was a plot
by brother officers to castrate my character.
Their words reeked with insults.
Even the blue mouth of sky gaped at their accusations.
My skin was a wall they kicked with hard heels of hate.

I'm not soliciting sympathy because of my color.
Because of my color, Lady Justice took off her blindfold,
unchained her scales, broke the blade of her sword across my back.
For years I have bled with dishonor.

How does a man bandage humiliation?
This letter is a plea to reinstate my pride with a pardon.
My name is a wall you can wash clean with the cloth of your pen,

John.

Loretta Diane Walker

In 1881, while serving at Fort Davis, Lt. Henry O. Flipper was dismissed from the Army. He wrote a letter to Representative John A. T. Hull, October 23, 1898, in an attempt to clear his name. The letter asks Congress for "that justice which every American citizen has the right to ask." In 1976, the Army granted him an honorable discharge, and in 1999, President Bill Clinton issued him a full pardon. ~ Center for Legislative Archives

Carl Hilmar Guenther (1826–1902), pioneer miller

Carl Hilmar Guenther

The Central Texas pioneers were growing grains but had no mill to grind them. Trained as a millwright I saw gains. A life among my fellow German immigrants drew me to Fredericksburg, a young and growing place. The scenic Pedernales River powered my first flour mill, yet one severe drought and a flood made me rebuild in San Antonio. There I ran Guenther's Mill for forty years, affording me a fine house and a family. When railroads came, I could expand into a larger region. In 1898 my youngest son joined me to carry on. Our growing firm, the doorstep of the 20th century, called for a broadened name. Remembering my early days we chose Pioneer Flour Mills.

in America
seize the opportunity
that presents itself

    Christa Pandey

The haiku in this haibun is a direct quote by C.H. Guenther, taken from information about the history of the Guenther House and Museum in San Antonio's King William District.

Hyman G. Neill/Hoodoo Brown (1856–1910), outlaw leader

Printer's Devil

Weren't no small feat headin' up my own gang
Took organ-*i*-zation and we made our mark, yes, sir!
Dodge City Gang, some called us vigilantes
It was business and sometimes self-defense I tell ya
Tender moments were rare, handy with the steel by my side
Not much time for proper courting
A few fillies came my way one in particular became
A merry widow whilst keeping company with a gentleman
Like myself. I aint no gee-tar pickin' troubadour
Many would call me ruthless, a gambler and a thief
Why some may label me worse
Known far and wide by my reputation
I wore many a hat to get by and contrary to popular belief
I too had dreams of grandeur when I opened that opry house in Mexico
Them was lawless times, so I took to a life of perilous crimes
Lexington to Colorado to Las Vegas, New Mexico
I'd sooner hop a train than settle in a one-horse town
Printer's devil, bison hunter, gambler, coroner and politician
I aint cut out for no regular life
No one can ever say "Hoodoo Brown ain't got no ambition!"

Jimmie Ware

Hoodoo Brown was an infamous figure of the old Southwest known for corruption as a career criminal politician and leader of the Dodge City Gang in the late 1800's. His life was filled with a wide array of "business endeavors" during a wild and lawless time.

Eunice Gray/Etta Place (1880–1962), brothel and hotel owner

Who's at the Waco Hotel?

They come each night, suits
with golden chains across fat bellies
paw and slobber on my girls
drop seed they won't put
in their tight-lipped bitter wives.

> He'd hit town stash and stable
> clean up at the barber's
> I'd wake to steps on wooden porch
> honeysuckle, bay rum and tobacco
> aroma as mattress slopes.

They make business deals in parlor
stumble half-drunk upstairs
leaning on laudanum-numbed women
grope and fiddle more used to climbing
on planks of rigid church women.

> In small, empty hours I feel
> pitch of mattress, callused hands
> he unlaces my nightdress, hand
> grips my thighs, he is safe
> and I can hardly draw my breath.

Sunlight warms hotel steps attracting
that snake, Norris, slithering slipping
his hand into Fort Worth's stuffed pockets
through fanfare and velvet-lined plates
He asks, *Have you heard of Jesus?*

> A whisky-soaked mustache brushes
> my neck as waterfall mist cools
> our bodies, he winks as agile fingers
> caress and tease; long hot time
> until dinner and we are hungry.

I should have shot him right
then, right there on the porch
but I tell him, *If Jesus comes by here
then me and my girls know him
real well.*

    Michelle Hartman

Though historians still argue the possibility of Eunice Gray being Etta Place, they cannot refute the finding of bank stock worth more than $90,000, in the walls of the Waco Hotel upon its demolition. Pinkerton detectives traced all of it back to jobs done by the Wild Bunch.

Gregorio Cortez Lira (1875–1916), farmer, folk hero

Canción de Cortez

trace the tracks of an alpha coyote
for eighty days in a windy plain

listen to dew drop from huizache
and roll into an arroyo

worry catalpa with bare fingers
until seed wings into mirage

lay down in a canyon and howl
to a black moon that you have lost me

take your hot swift irons and wistful guns
your frayed-end ropes and gumless hounds

take your empty trails full of misgiving
your ragged steeds and bow-legged mares

take them to your capitol
and lay them down

take them to your words of paper
and burn them like dried leaves

take them to your virgen de justicia
and raise her white flag

and perhaps if I wish
you can find me there

brilliant beneath an oppressor's gaze
brazen in judgment of my stolen life

    Wade Martin

Gregorio Cortez Lira was a Mexican-American tenant farmer who became a folk hero after a 10-day, 500-mile flight from over 300 law enforcers (one of the largest manhunts in history). He is also said to have pleaded the court for a fair trial untainted by racism.

canción: song; virgen de justicia: virgin of justice

Henry Wickenburg (1819–1905), prospector

Sign

I can still see the iron-stained quartz
with its placer vein —
the outcrop up by Antelope Creek —
and remember believing it was my salvation,
though it surely was more Satan's work
than God's.

Half my life ago I staked my claim
on Vulture Mine, and all but four years since
I've wasted on it. Not a judge
in this Territory's wise enough
to see past the lies about my title
to the claim, and I'd wager more than one
took a little gold on the side
to grease his judgment.

I'm ashamed to set foot in the church
I built, ashamed of my worn coat,
the hole in my boot. I see
the widows' pitying eyes.

And no matter what the Reverend says,
I won't forgive those bastards their sins.
When I was a judge, I hung many a high-grader
for stealing less than a hundredth
what those swindlers took from me.

The day I heaved that gold-seamed stone
at vultures circling over my head,
I should have taken them for a sign —
what comes when a man has wealth,
drawn to the poison of a festering wound.

Cindy Huyser

The town of Wickenburg, Arizona, was named for Prussian immigrant Johannes Henricus "Henry" Wickenburg. Over the years, he served as a judge, justice of the peace, and a member of the seventh Territorial Legislature, and he also funded the irrigation project that led to the establishment of Phoenix. He was 44 years old in 1863 when he staked his claim on the lode that became the Vulture Mine; a New York firm bought the claim from him in 1866 for $85,000, but paid him $20,000, then contested his clear title and refused to pay the rest. Wickenburg would spend the rest of his life in fruitless legal battles with the company. Destitute and in poor health, Wickenburg died an apparent suicide on May 14, 1905.

Mary Hunter Austin (1868–1934), nature writer

Motherhood, Desert

I've known men
      who think the sands and mountains inert,
           easy to conquer and own.

And what does the arid wind do?
      Tears them down. Dries them up.
           Turns them to carrion.

I once dreamed of you
      like foolish explorers dream
           of controlling landscape.

Ruth, you were born
      a sandstorm,
           a drought.

My arms were no use as shelter.
      My body ran out of nourishment.
           My mind could not comprehend how to nurture you.

This territory has dried
      me up, my resolve
           cracking like parched skin.

Allyson Whipple

Mary Hunter Austin was an activist who wrote a prolific number of books, essays, and other works, primarily on environmental topics. Her only child was born with a severe mental handicap, and after a failed marriage, years of troubled finances, and her own health issues, Austin reluctantly surrendered her daughter to an institution.

Elizabeth McCourt "Baby Doe" Tabor (1854–1935), society patron

The Post-Feminist Ramblings of Baby Doe Tabor's Ghost

Do you think you can tell it better
than I can? Others have called me
doe-eyed and beautiful; a gold-digging
home wrecker; spendthrift; slut; worthless
mother of ill-gotten girls; the crazy woman
who died half-naked and penniless, frozen
into the shape of the cross on the cabin
floor they plied me from, burying
me next to the man I stole from a woman
he never did love. But that's just half my story.
What remains are all the reasons I still haunt
this ghost town, all the words I wrote down on scraps
I hoarded like the silver that made me so rich
once, dripping in ermine and jewels. Don't you
hear the sound of my footsteps as I wander
these streets wrapped in rags?

Margaret Dornaus

Elizabeth McCourt "Baby Doe" Tabor was the second wife of wealthy Colorado silver magnate Horace Tabor. Her rags-to-riches-to-rags story made her a well-known figure during her lifetime, and later inspired an opera and a Hollywood movie.

Sylvia Ridley (1870–1905), Choctaw woman

Papers in a Vanishing Room

1905. Durant, Choctaw Nation, Indian Territory

Dearest K —

You'll remember, I used to draw butterflies
where I wanted to cut. Not anymore.
Maybe you have heard.

> *The* Sulphur Post *says SYLVIA RIDLEY INSANE*
> *Sylvia Ridley, an Indian woman of 35 years of age,*
> *became violently insane Tuesday. She was taken to*
> *Ardmore under arrest. She was tried Monday,*
> *January 2, at Marietta, and sent to the asylum.*

I am getting well. Just this morning, I woke
and for a moment thought I was home (but then
all in a panic because I could not find the children).
At night: I imagine the smell of our squash blossoms filling my room.
Then, my hands and my mouth and my throat and my wrists
peel open, unwhorl like squash blossoms —
my ears go off, my eyes, my fingers float away.
From the holes flow the moons you taught me to name,
moons sifting across the white floors
shadow patterns, as precise as spiders':
the green corn moon, the worm moon,
the beautiful long night's moon.

> *The woman had been married three times; her first two*
> *husbands, Indians, died, and Ridley, a white man, left*
> *her, got a divorce, and married again. It is supposed*
> *that worry over these facts led to her dementia.*

For years our people wandered, carrying the bones of their dead
until they found a place to lay them.

Even today, we are returned home,
placed upon a litter, covered in skins and bark,
provisioned with food and drink, a killed dog
for companionship. And after some weeks,
the bone-picker comes and scrapes the flesh away
with his long fingernails. So we can always know this.

> *She had been about Sulphur for the last four or five*
> *months, working at one place and another, but never*
> *staying long.*

All I said was that I know there is God, but
I also think to grandmother's stories of *Nalusa chito*,
the Great Black Thing, how if I gave into the sadness,
Nalusa chito would crawl through my skin and eat my soul.
Do you remember when you would laugh at me for crying?
I forgive you for that now.
There is a woman here who frightens me.
Her name is Yells-at-Night.
I believe I will see you soon.

Love, S.R.

J. Todd Hawkins

In January 1905, Sylvia Ridley, a Choctaw woman, was sent from Oklahoma to the Hiawatha Asylum for Insane Indians in South Dakota. Confinement at the asylum was often used as retribution against mentally healthy Native Americans who had irritated Indian agents or local politicians. Even for the standards of the time, conditions were deplorable at the institution, where inmates were restrained for extended periods, forced to live in filth, and denied basic needs. In June, Ridley died. She is buried in the old asylum cemetery, which is today located between the fourth and fifth fairways of the Hiawatha Golf Club. "Papers in a Vanishing Room" contains found elements: the italicized and indented stanzas consist of text from the January 4, 1905, issue of the Tishomingo News (Oklahoma).

Bass Reeves (1838–1910), Deputy U.S. Marshal

Bass Reeves, Deputy U. S. Marshal

They want me to talk about my life
now that it's mos' over.
I reckon I can do that.
Folks that knows me know I'm a talker.
I have bragged some
but I figger this ain't the time for that.
I been called all sorts a' names
some nicer'n others but I never paid much mind.
With my size, the badge, and a hard look
they mos'ly got polite n' I never figgered
what they said to my back mattered much.
The Lord said we's all neighbors.
I tried to 'member that even with all them folks
I arrested in thirty-two years of badge wearin'.
I never tried to keep count but they say it was
more'n three thousand. Don't seem possible.
I mos'ly tried to catch'm by surprise
to make it easy for all o' us but
fourteen had to go to Judgement
'cuz they tried to make a fight of it.

I reckon it's my turn for that last trip.
Least that's what the doc says.
It was comforting when my son
read to me from the paper
what the folk I worked with
had to say 'bout me.
It was good stuff 'bout how hard I worked
and how I never handed in the wrong warrant
even though I couldn't read the names.
I learnt'm when they read them to me.
I'se proud of that and mos' all I did.
Family thought I should quit
chasin' bad guys and riskin' my life

but I couldn't stop doin' what I was good at.
It was important n' I was respected.
I kinda figgered I was doin'
the work the Good Lord give me
and it's hard to beat that.

It's not a lot a' fellers born slaves
that get such kind things said
by all them white officers,
n' judges, n' lawyers.

It ain't easy a'layin' here
waitin' for the dark
but I reckon I did 'bout the best I could
n' reckon it'll have to do.

Del Cain

Bass Reeves was born into slavery in Arkansas in 1838. His owners, the Reeves family, moved to northeast Texas where, during the Civil War, Bass ran away into Indian Territory, learned the land, people, and many of their languages. In 1875 he was recruited to become a Deputy U. S. Marshal in the court of Judge Isaac Parker. He served the Marshal's Service for thirty-two years.

Swift Fox/Willie Boy (1881–1909 or –1933), Paiute fugitive

Swift Fox Is Here

Tell them
Tell them all —

Tell the whites
who call me Willie Boy
like I'm one of them —

That's not my name.

Tell the movie moguls
who pester my spirit
so they can line their pockets —

Tell the Indian haters
who can't face the shame
of a failed posse —

Tell the man who shot
my love in the back
because she wore my jacket,

then said I killed her
to keep her from
slowing me down —

Tell everyone who thinks
the law caught me or shot me
or I killed myself —

Tell them all
I'm outside the law —

My people know this
and hold my secret

My birthplace knows this
and holds my secret

Every rock of the land
I traveled knows this
and holds my secret —

How I ran north
reached my home
and lived on

while the deputies
posed with a corpse
they called mine —

Tell the grifters
who argue my fate

Tell them
Tell them all —

Ghost dancers
never die.

    Cynthia Anderson

The official version of the Willie Boy story states that after killing his lover's father, he ran off with her into the hills above Banning, California, killing both her and himself during the manhunt (1909). However, new evidence supports the outcome always held by the Native Americans as true: the young woman was shot by the posse, and Willie Boy, aka Swift Fox, escaped and lived with his people in Nevada.

Adina Amelia de Zavala (1861–1955), preservationist

Remember the Alamo

I am determined to stay.
No food — no water —
night of the second day.

My fellow Daughters
smuggle food, water —
enough to keep me alive.
My fellow Daughters
weep and sigh —
pray to keep me alive.

Old bricks and rats
weep and sigh
as I huddle against drafts.
Old bricks and rats
all the company I keep
while they draw up draughts
to tear down this old Keep.

Companies of police keep
friends and family away
from this worn down old Keep
worried I'll convince them to stay.
But my family friends are away
this night of the second day.

If I can't convince them —
I am determined to stay.

Wade Martin

Adina Emilia De Zavala, a preservationist, led efforts to save the Alamo Long Barrack Fortress. On February 10, 1908, De Zavala entered the Long Barrack alone and without provision, successfully holding a three-day occupation to prevent commercial interests from tearing that portion of the Alamo down.

Annie Oakley/Phoebe Ann Mosey (1860–1926), sharpshooter

Dear Your Honor Kind Sir Kaiser Wilhelm II

October 20, 1914

Do you remember? Remember how you called me Phoebe?
My given name, a'course, though long-ago shucked,
almost forgotten. But you, daft for myth and myth-making
saw in me: Phoebe-Artemis-Diana the Huntress. Not with
a bow, nossir, but with a gun. Yes, I who'd become a girl
of the Wild West, with a man's hat, long rat-tail of hair,
and medals across my chest.

Remember how chuffed you were by my strong arms and
splay-foot stance? You weren't exactly fresh with me,
yet you teased 'til I said I'd shoot the ash off your cigarette.
Done. A bang-up success. Then you called me Moon Goddess
and bussed me twice on each cheek.

Now, it seems, you're tail over teakettle in the middle
of a great war, and this is the second letter I've written you
since mid-summer. I would like another chance to shoot at
your ash. Why aren't you answering? What is it you're
afeared of? Would I, your Diana, presume to hurt you?

Yours with humility and ambition, Phoebe Ann Mosey
aka Annie Oakley

Susan Terris

Annie Oakley did, indeed, shoot the ash of the cigarette of Kaiser William II (then Prince Wilhelm) of Germany, about 1890 or 1891. After World War I broke out, many joked that if Annie had missed, maybe the war would never have taken place. The letter above is imaginative fiction.

West Texas settler (circa 1900–1940)

Kerosene

Burns intensely hot, but is safe.
Them slick ads in Ladies Journal
promised that kerosene stoves
were *blessings that led to fewer*
and happier hours in the kitchen.
Under Mama's kettles and pots,
the flames glowed blue as rainless
sky, and that bitter winter,
quick as you please, they melted
ice I'd hacked from the cistern,
so's to sieve it, then start the mush,
while Daddy murmured, struggling
from bed, wore out by arthritis.

That night before the fire,
before Mama piled on quilts enough
to smother me and Sister,
before our wood-frame home
went cold, shook and creaked,
Daddy added fuel to fill
the stove's glass crock,
bucket-sized, that fed the burners.
So's you don't run out, he said.

Run out I did, that dawn,
dragging Sister like a rag doll
when melting ice boiled over,
cracked the glass. The kerosene
spilled, lit up, then torched
the greasy floor. Ma fought the flames
with a mop, Daddy stomped.

My screams roused the crows
who soared through the smoke
then floated like cinders.

Marilyn Westfall

The narrator is the daughter of settlers in West Texas where, in sparsely populated counties, electrical service wasn't established until after World War II. Kerosene stoves were common appliances. Diarists and journalists recorded fires and deaths that resulted from fuel spills, sometimes when children were in charge of the cooking. The incident is based on a fire that blazed in Clairemont, Texas, and the town was in its heyday from the late 1800s through 1957. The model of kerosene stove was available for purchase around 1915 or so.

George McJunkin (1851–1922), cowboy

Waiting for Sunlight

Words are tougher to read
Than cows, I cyphered them out
With kind folks' help, then
Rode into books and drove cows
To ranches with hoof beats

My fingers on bones and violin strings
Played where above the Cimarron
The earth's packed layers split
Dusty Dead Horse arroyo and
The '08 storm tore fence and time

Chiseled points stuck in ribs
Too-big for buffalo called
Come here George, look
You know some old bone
Tales, tell us to someone

I know men with letters
Can talk to bones so I
Wrote them, They're age-soaked
Bones heavy with time
Come see a new story

But a dark cow man is only
Land shadows no weight
He don't know things
Just bones still moving
Caballos and vacas

Now time washes o'er me like
Another Folsom flood 'n I hear
Those old bones call me *Come*
Join us Soon we'll read you our
Secrets in the New Mexico lands

Kegged up in town too weak to move
A pard reads the Good Book's
Stories of ones who've gone before
Layers of ownership, cruel slavery
Compressing their wise old bones

But freedom is near I know
I'll join the gone-befores and
Turned-to-stone giants then
Together we'll rest old buffalo
Bones waiting for sunlight.

   Nancy Fine

George McJunkin, born 1856, was a well-respected black New Mexico ranch foreman. A self-taught man fluent in Spanish, he collected books, played violin, and along with other accomplishments became an amateur archeologist. Although he discovered the Folsom Point site — an archeological find that moved man's arrival in North America back 7,000 years — he could not, in his lifetime, persuade professionals to visit the site.

caballos: horses; vacas: cows

Phoenix Indian School (1891–1931)

Phoenix Indian School

My walls are made of the same brown earth that birthed their savage
    bodies.
They come to me reluctant, full of fight, bucking like wild horses.
I eat their untamed spirits, solstice hearts,
cud and collapse them like wine.

I whip defiant skin,
clip dark manes into something presentable,
cover bodies in suits and petticoats,
black dresses empty of beads.

My stone makes feet forget the feel of the
earth, curve against words like shoe.
Headdress is Hat. Navajo is Nathan.
Names are only needed by the living.

I collect brothers, sisters, cousins.
They whisper in tongues older than time.
I know the secrets no one can hear.
Too many ears to count.

I pull children in, crumple chalk dust eyes
and damn them to pray for salvation.
I grab them in dreams, shifting their shapes.
They wake almost beautiful.

Fatima-Ayan Malika Hirsi and Wade Martin

Phoenix Indian School operated from 1891 until 1931 under the federal government's "assimilation" program, designed to exterminate Native American culture. It became Phoenix Indian High School in 1931 and closed its doors in 1990.

To the End of the Millennium (1919–1999)

J. Frank Norris (1877–1952), Baptist preacher

In the center ring sensationalistic preaching

And what to do with Norris was a question broad and deep.
He was too big to banish, and he smelled too bad to keep.
       ~ an old Baptist poem

Barnum had nothing on me,
three rings going, with clowns
performing wonders on the sides.
Southern Baptists were too modern;
murder was not too messy.

So I was shady in my back room dealings.
I brought religion up to the big show.
Airplanes, newspapers and radio shows
owned by a church are nothing new.

I was Godfather of all that is holy
and wholly repugnant, a master pulpiteer
who called out rich and powerful alike.
I gave them blazing-hot summer nights
fraught with fervor and entertainment.

When I left this mortal coil
my pall bearers were members of my treasury committee.
Just shows you the best religious lesson:
if you cannot take it with you
you can at least have it carry you out.

   Michelle Hartman

John Franklyn (J. Frank) Norris (September 18, 1877–August 20, 1952) was a flamboyant Baptist preacher and a controversial Christian fundamentalist. He is considered the father of "Big Time Religion."

Ormer Locklear (1891–1920), daredevil stunt pilot

The Wing Walker

Records are set and broken,
reset, broken again,

just like fliers' bones.
Men die learning to fly

here in Texas,
and the life expectancy

of a fighter pilot overseas?
Three weeks.

I climb out of the cockpit,
my partner takes the controls,

I walk the lower wing,
do handstands on the top.

Pickens heard about our stunts,
signed me and my pals,

Skeets and Shorty,
to wing-walk *rain, shine, or cyclone,*

in Uniontown, Erie, and Atlantic City,
a thousand dollars a show.

He bills us as a circus,
three miles long and a mile high.

When I fell he said,
Bandages are box office.

Dolores Hayden

Ormer Locklear (1891–1920), born in Greenville, near Fort Worth, was a military flight instructor in Texas who invented the wing-walk. His co-pilot took the controls while Locklear climbed up on the wings of their Curtiss Jenny biplane to walk the wings and do other acrobatic stunts. Locklear was recruited by William Hickman Pickens, a promoter who arranged for the Locklear Flying Circus — Locklear and two friends — to wing-walk at state fairs. Wing-walking soon became a craze, and under Pickens' guidance, Locklear was one of the first stunt pilots hired to work in silent movies in Hollywood. He died in a crash filming the last scene of The Skywayman. *Source: Ronnie, Art,* Locklear: The Man Who Walked on Wings.

Chipeta/White Singing Bird (circa 1843–1924), Native rights advocate

Chipeta

I am Moache, Capote, Weeminuche, White River,
and Timpanogot, with whom I shared this land,
these rivers and the peaks of the Rocky Mountains.
I am Uncompahgre of the Ute tribe, wife of Chief Ouray,
Tabegauche, of the Uncomgahgre River Valley,
the Elk Mountains.

I am White Singing Bird, Kiowa Apache baby raised
by the Ute tribe. I am a sixteen-year-old bride playing
on my beautiful guitar, singing in three languages and telling
stories in the white man's tongue of trappers, overwhelmed
by newcomers, miners, farmers, pioneers, who took the
hunting grounds, shrinking them year by year.

When the White Rivers killed Agent Meeker, I rescued the women
and children, sheltered them in my tent, by my fire. When they took
us to Alamosa, I felt the rope grow tight around my neck before
they rescued me and Ouray made his mark on the white man's piece
of paper. It was I who gave little George, the poor little frightened
white boy, his new name — Uviev, *walks like a turkey.*

I am Chipeta, the only woman of my tribe to sit in the council
of my people, or go by train to visit the White Father in his faraway
land where they called me, without derision, the Queen of the Utes.
Now I am the widow of Ouray. Year by year, decade by decade,
the census taker writes *Uncompahgre* by my name, but nothing else.

The history books of Colorado leapfrog from Francisco Domingues,
1776, to the laying out of Montrose. They speak of truck farms,
potatoes, sweet corn, onions, pinto beans, lettuce, peppers
and tomatoes. But in this fertile land, I am banished
half a century to pine for my people, then abandoned at the
White Rocks in Uintah, my bones in my grave, small and white.

McCook, my brother, has come to take me home. At last, he comes to honor me, White Bird, Chipeta the Peacemaker.

Dawnell H. Griffin

The speaker in this persona poem is the historical character, Chipeta, wife of Chief Ouray of the Uncompahgre Ute Tribe. She was a remarkable and intelligent woman, honored by both her tribe and the white people with whom she mediated in behalf of the Utes.

Roscoe Platt Conkling (1877–1971), explorer, author

Overland: Roscoe, July 1926

Disgraced, the leering broadsheets jeer, torn letter from
a roving mining engineer the ruinous clue that proves
why Brewster shot his wife then killed himself.
                                                                        But I,
dear Tracy, stray animal of *Santa Ana*,
grieve only for one moonlit April second, three
nights out from port, Beethoven from my violin,
soft talk, shipboard companionship, a birthday cake;
if these a love triangle make then I am damned.
Divorced, disowned, abettor of a deuce of deaths,
I'll flee. Parral's no safer since Villa's murder;
Manhattan's made for madness; Catskill's closed.
                                                                       Why not
look north, ASARCO's border city? El Paso,
as passable asylum as a gringo's apt
to find: convenient for entradas, Spanish friars,
the westbound stage, the Bankhead, tales of buried gold.
The past a pastime to be mined, a place to hide;
romance enough to keep a seeker occupied
when every other joy he cared about has died.

    Barbara Brannon

Historians of the American Southwest know New York native Roscoe Platt Conkling and his second wife, Margaret Badenoch Vear, a piano teacher from Chicago, as the chroniclers of the Butterfield Overland Trail, the nation's first transcontinental mail and stagecoach route in the years prior to the Civil War.

entradas: expeditions

Margaret Badenoch Vear Conkling (1890–1973), teacher

Overland: Margaret, June 1930

I traveled to the desert with a lunger from
Chicago. Charles Vear, my dear departed husband,
didn't live a year. How strange it was to see us
in the city book between Vasquez and Vega.
But I sent his body home, and stayed, a widow
giving lessons for a dime. El Paso suited
me. It needed music, and I had it to give.

Roscoe was another matter. My match and more,
conductor sans portfolio, Dvořák on
the border, cave explorer (did you know he led
an oratorio once, underground?). Deep in
the Organ Mountains, where the miners say the gold
was buried in the Bishop's Cap, Roscoe and I
were married. Top that!
                        Soon we will; the old trail calls.
Overland we go, across the wide Missouri
and the Red, the Pecos and the Rio Grande.
Following the faintest trace of phantom driver,
making our own map our modus operandi,
we resurrect the Butterfield's former glory.
Mind you, history will live on in this story.

Barbara Brannon

Few know details of the Conklings' separate lives before they first crossed paths in El Paso, Texas — division point of the Butterfield, and the city that became home base of their grand adventure by car during the height of the Great Depression. Scandal seemed to hound the restless Roscoe until he settled down with another adoptive Southwesterner in a city that offered sanctuary to sojourners including fugitives and friars, tubercular patients, and not least, artists and seekers.

Wyatt Earp (1848–1929), frontiersman

Wyatt Earp Writes His Final Diary Entry

for my grandfather, Grover Cleveland "Snap" Foster

I'm a man of few words — even fewer written words — but I ain't dead yet and I want to make something clear. Going to Tombstone was the worst decision of my life.

But they'd found silver there, and my brothers and I had good prospects. I did it all — sold real estate, rode shotgun for Wells Fargo, managed poker tables at the Oriental Saloon. Then the murderers, thieves, cattle rustlers, and rapists who called themselves cowboys maimed my older brother and gunned down my younger brother Morgan, shooting him in the back from a dark alley. They threatened and leered at our wives.

I was a law-abiding man, but the judge treated as gospel the alibis of those killers, the testimony of their no-count friends infesting that courtroom — all liars. Everybody knowed the lot of them should have been thrown in the hoosegow and hanged the next morning. Instead they walked away scot-free. I'd been deputized and knew the law, but that blamed judge from back east didn't do squat-doodle.

So I did it myself. I caught up with the last of them at the train station trying to hightail it out of town. The coward who'd gunned down Morgan knelt between the tracks begging for his life. As the night train shot in, it hid us from folks on the platform. Nobody heard him scream. It weren't no silver bullet I put through his head.

Adrenaline is my muse — it affects me different from other men. My blood, my brain freeze into something as calculating and deafening as sterling so that my hands steady and my eyes illumine. I'm no gunslinger, but my aim is always on the money.

In the dark I slid like quicksilver onto the train bound for California. I was still a young man in a boom town back then, and I'd be damned if I didn't kill the wild old west before it killed me.

Aletha Irby

Wyatt Earp is an American hero and a national treasure, although I think he himself would have denied it. The Old West was a tough training ground, even for a man with the proverbial "nerves of steel," or in this case, silver. I like to think that every American has a little of Wyatt Earp in them.

Migrant mother (circa 1930)

From El Valle to West Texas: Following la Cosecha

Julio, Agosto, Septiembre, we stuffed and emptied our cotton
sacks, fingers torn, the sun stealing our bent breath. Then
the relentless pains arrived, still far away from la pisca in Lubbock.
Too soon . . . too soon . . .

You wrenched yourself out of me in the back of la troca,
la colcha blood-drenched. Ay, Diosito! Your tiny body
barely pulsed in my arms, skin flutter-thin, your head
cupped como huevito in my palm. A few moments . . .

then not even a whisper of breath — nada.
I cradled you against my chest junto a mi corazón,
held onto you until the others plucked you from me.
They wrapped you in Memo's clean shirt,

nestled you in the dry earth, buried you on the side
of the road — only the brush and bluestems left
to sing to you. Mi corazón y alma quebrados,
I named you María de la Luz, mi preciosa bebita.

My breasts leaked for weeks even though I bound
them with cloth. We couldn't have returned
to our casita en Mercedes, had to leave you on that lonely
strip of road under the vast blanket of sky,

had to heed the call of the white bolls erupting
from hulls — their own ripening time.
Had to earn money for the long stretch,
la renta, comida, todo. . . .

Noviembre, la pisca over, and we returned
to El Valle, my arms barren, picked clean.
I kept looking for the rise of earth
where we buried you. . . .

Ayyy, mi Luz — mi Lucita —
Only I will remember your name.

   Gloria Amescua

The migrant mother in this poem is inspired by a family story. She is one of the thousands of workers in the Southwest who endured many hardships following the crops. In the early part of the 20th century, the majority were Mexican and Mexican Americans. I have written poems about individuals whose names would not be found in history — though I have done a great deal of research to write these poems. They are individuals who represent many people important to the culture, history and diversity of the Southwest. I believe their lives created what we know of the Southwest, though they remained unnamed.

la Cosecha: the Harvest; la pisca: the picking; la colcha: the quilt; como huevito: like a little egg; junto: next to; Mi corazón y alma quebrados: My heart and soul broken; la renta, comida, todo: the rent, food, everything

William Evans (circa 1888–1935), carnival operator

For the Correction of History

Yes, the six-legged sheep and the dog-faced calf
are lovely in their way. But for you, something . . . different.
Let me tell you this: I have a mummy.
Come closer, yes, closer. . . .
He is real, and you may see him for yourself
for just two bits. Look:

the brow scar, a misplaced swordblow from *Richard III*;
the crooked thumb, crushed in a curtain windlass long ago;
and of course the twisted leg, so crudely set by Dr. Mudd.
I know each crease. I comb his moustache, polish his marble eyes.
And at night, I slick his leather limbs with Vaseline
till he glistens like scarab wings in a black desert.

I sleep next to him in the panel truck,
we two showmen, we two curators of dead legends.
These days, I never leave his side.
For once in San Diego, he was kidnapped, ransomed,
and in Salt Lake City, I fled in the dark —
the sheriff after me for teaching a false history.

In Big Spring, they fined me for harboring a corpse.
They tried to bury my Johnny. As if their own lives
were so genuine; their own stupid stories, veritable.
It is enough to make me want to stay out here forever, to show
my relics before the cactus cloaked in powdered stone,
the buzzards minding their private bones.

Yes, even the damn buzzards would be better audience —
I hit one on the way here as it gorged on day-dead rabbit,
swollen with heat, and it splashed into unwashable crevices of the Ford.
I cursed and laughed for miles. But the final laugh is theirs,
for any way out of here or into here feels forever gone now,
and the buzzards, from the ground, are sublime and holy.

Or perhaps I will learn to float with them
through yellow rivers of dust in sun,
dancing with the cottonwood plumes,
and leave my two-faced kitten — precious Janus! —
my pickled punks and feegee mermaid,
and, yes, even my Booth —

Leave him there, on the roadside, the withered pharaoh,
leave him, clothed in corroborations, dressed in affidavits,
propped on plywood
for the correction of history.
Leave him here, disentranced
with his own pretended permanence.

   J.Todd Hawkins

In 1903, a Shakespeare-quoting drifter named David George committed suicide in Enid, Oklahoma, but not before confessing to being Abraham Lincoln's assassin, John Wilkes Booth. George's body was embalmed and placed on display at the Enid funeral parlor until it could be claimed by the government or his nearest kin. The mummy became an Enid tourist attraction and eventually fell into the hands of William Evans, "Carnival King of the Southwest," who exhibited the Booth mummy throughout the West for many years as a carnival attraction.

Carrie Elizabeth Zimpleman Williams (1884–1936), Texas transplant

Damp to Dust

Oneida's come to care for me and brought
her cold. It seeps through my thinning skin, slips
down my throat. Yet peace reigns in our red-rose
room. From the bed I can watch my children
walk to school. Each day James whispers ...
      My Dutch doll.

It was 1916 when I abandoned
Indiana for dry country. A cure. Long,
clacking days on trains — apple orchards
in Missouri, small corn in Kansas.
In Texas, I wrote in my journal ...
      Unfamiliar energy has filled my porous lungs.

October now, the dusty cotton-picking
season. In a rising fever, I relive
opening the door to James, his fingers
clutching a white Stetson — ranch hand, widower
with small children. His jealous mother sniping ...
      Fortune hunter!

Oneida brings me broth with bits of chicken,
vegetables she's cut. With little money,
but plenty of thread and love, I've feather-stitched
a life as fine as my quilts. Survived
the birth of our three sons and a daughter ...
      Why should I not have what other women do?

And music! I finger the keys and stops
of the pump organ my father shipped,
my fair-haired daughter pushing the pedals.
We entertain the pastor when he comes
to bless and savor my butterscotch pie ...
      A holy creation this, Carrie Elizabeth!

I don't regret the Texas Panhandle.
Twenty years it's given me. More than
Indiana's rolling green damp could have done.
James sits helpless by my side, my fever
resisting interference. The doctor
affirming what he's said would someday come.

Sandi Stromberg

Carrie Elizabeth Zimpleman Williams was my maternal grandmother, who traveled alone from Indiana and a cultured, artistic life to the unknown wilds of the Texas Panhandle in hopes of finding a cure for her severe asthma. She died at age 52 in Kress, Texas.

Miyoshi Jingu (1893–1969), hostess, actress

Teahouse of the Texas Moon

There is nothing you can think that is not the moon.
  ~ Matsuo Basho

Your silvered glow, San Antonio moon,
spills like a billion stars.

Under your cool fire,
I count hours, if lucky, days.
Where will we go?
That faraway city,
named for crystal
but adorned with barbed wire?

My eight young
who yesterday splashed among lily pads
long for their artist father
as if five years passed in five nights.
Beneath your piercing eye, I lie:
  We will be all right.

What to take? My mother's kimono of red silk?
To warm us, some earthy Matcha tea?
This small painting by Kimi, snow
white peony luminous through cobalt glaze?
Or from our pond, lotus
like a sleeping angel?

Gratitude of guests now gone?
  This tea is refreshing, Miyoshi.
    Your children, so sweet — especially Mabel.

In December's damp chill,
I pray to you, gibbous god,
my hope thin as rice paper.

Let me be quicksilver,
shift, change,
move as fluidly as indigo watercolor.

Under your lunar light,
Pearl Harbor.
Will mercy rise
for those who shout at us
      Leave now — and don't look back?

Wandering Sister, who never failed my sky-bent prayers,
will you return to fullness?
Seed the river's face with iridescent pearls?

   Linda Simone

In 1926, the City of San Antonio invited Miyoshi Alice Jingu and her artist-husband Kimi to run the teahouse at its new Japanese Garden. Within fifteen years, Miyoshi and her children, once called a "unique asset" by the San Antonio Express, *would be forced out of their teahouse home as "enemy aliens."*

Chester Nez (1921–2014), Navajo code talker

Chester Nez Arriving at Guadalcanal, 1942

   TANK
      CHAY-DA-GAHI
         TORTOISE

   BATTLESHIP
      LO-TSO
         WHALE

   AIRCRAFT
      TSIDI-MOFFA-YE-HI
         BIRD CARRIER

   SUBMARINE
      BESH-LO
         IRON FISH

   MINE SWEEPER
      CHA
         BEAVER

   DESTROYER
      CA-LO
         SHARK

   BOMB
      A-YE-SHI
         EGG

   CRUISER
      LO-TSO-YAZZIE
         SMALL WHALE

         ~ Navajo Code Talkers' Dictionary *(rev., 1945)*

Tanks become tortoises   submarines iron fish   bombs eggs
military-entities we've never seen on the reservation
    Roy and I fill with fear to our chests
    cranking up the radio for power
    for our first transmission

our people are warriors   we wanted to defend America
with courage and spirit as Navajo Marines
we stitched our unpapered language to English alphabet letters
making two hundred code words this war cannot enter
thirty-two of us worried that any error could cost the life of a comrade
we kept the codes under our pillows to absorb in sleep
Roy and I would talk of our families in Chichiltah
rimmed by powdery red rocks blanketed by clouds
coaxed to rest there by the endless blue across time
the baby sheep and kids wearing tinkle bells
adults with small cow bells chiming the desert
echoing across purple-red mesas   we'd drift off
not knowing we'd endure days without food in a shifting sand hole
days ago thirteen of us filled our last supper plates
with battle apprehension and over-cooked meatloaf
before climbing down the many crosses of a net
into waiting pocket-boats convulsing on dark Pacific waters

    The wind answers back and we'll remember
    the first answer-code transmittal as long as we breathe

    We understand

Jan La Roche

Chester Nez was born January 23, 1921, and died June 4, 2014. He was a Navajo Code Talker from New Mexico, who served in the U.S. Marine Corps during World War II in Guadalcanal, Bougainville, Guam, Anguar, and Peleliu. He and thirty-two other Navajo Marines created two hundred code words, in their language, that the Japanese could not break. He received a Gold Medal from President Bush in 2001. The movie, Windtalkers, *with Nicolas Cage (2002) is a direct portrayal of Nez's experiences in the war. His book,* Code Talker: The First and Only Memoir by One of the Original Navajo Code Talkers of WWII *(2011) tells his story and also highlights the contributions and sacrifices of the Navajo in World War II.*

Peter MacDonald (1928–), Navajo code talker, politician

Navajo Code Talker

They came to us
diné bilágaana —the white guys
in uniforms juniper green — U.S. Marines
told us we were needed by our country
to fight the Japs and confuse the enemy
they sent a bus to Shiprock
just boys, some of us got on board

I was thinking all the way to Gallup
when was it our country?
when the Spanish horsemen
left all for dead in Massacre Cave?
when Colonel Carson and the army came for us
and our people walked the Long Walk
freezing, starving in the snow
from Canyon de Chelly to Bosque Redondo?
when the Indian Bureau came and slaughtered most of our sheep?
was it our country then?

It was a long way from Kayenta to Guadalcanal
from Teec Nos Pos to Iwo Jima
from the ship's decks no d'zil — our four sacred mountains — to be
          seen
I wore my turquoise nuggets to remind me of the ya dootł'izh
the blue skies of the Kaibito
they sent us to Okinawa —
382nd Platoon, 4th Division, U.S. Marine Corps —
we set up our radios, sent our messages to
our other diné brothers — who told the brass
then would come the artillery, rockets, mortars, planes

The Japanese hated us
could not break the codes in Navajo language — diné biz'aad
even Tokyo Rose cussed us out

told us to ditch those Americans
"boys, come on over to see me..."
we would be treated like royalty
we laughed — she made promises just like the teachers
in the agency schools — be good and you won't get a whipping!

It was war. We did our part.
We used our strong language —
the language they told us not to speak in school —
funny how they found it useful after all
but that was many years ago.
Soon not one of us remains.

   Gordon L. Magill

The speaker in this poem is Navajo Code Talker and U.S. Marine Corps veteran Peter MacDonald, who much later became first Tribal Chairman of the Navajo Nation, Arizona. The poem also includes ideas and imagery from several other Navajo Code Talkers I researched, including Chester Nez, Joe Vandever, and Samuel Tso, as well as from my own interview of a Navajo Code Talker for an exhibit I wrote on Navajo culture for New Mexico State Parks.

diné bilágaana: white people; d'zil: mountains; ya dootł'izh: blue skies; Kaibito: the vast plateau that comprises much of the Navajo land; diné: Navajo; diné biz'aad: Navajo language

Japanese internees (circa 1943)

Dai-dōrō in the Desert

Hot, dry, desolate. Cactus. Sagebrush. Jackrabbit holes. Rattlesnakes. Wind. Nothing like California.

Flat, as far as I see at first. Mountains in the far west. I know it is west because there the sun sets.

Sand becomes fine dust under our thousand feet. The beauty of the sand storm rolls towards us. Then, dust, dust, dust. Always sweeping. It enters any crack.

They made us eat salt pills. We dug a hole under the barracks to escape the heat.

"Are you human?" a young soldier asks. Don't you think so? "They told me Japs are like gorillas, and so you can kill them. But you look human; you wear beautiful clothes." I had one paper suitcase, good clothes only. This, the only country we know.

Some young men cut the barbed wire at night to hunt rabbits. We walk on the American desert, dispossessed.

stone lantern
in the green-less desert
our victory garden

Katherine Durham Oldmixon

---

dai-dōrō: a platform lamp used in gardens and along the approach to a shrine or temple

---

A gathering of voices and images, remembering the Japanese internment at Poston, Arizona; Gila River, Arizona; Topaz, Utah, and Heart Mountain, Wyoming:

    Chiyoko Yagi
    George Yoshinaga
    Gloria Kubota
    Grace Oshita
    K. Morgan Yamanaka
    Mitsuko Hashiguchi
    Mollie Nakasaki
    Mutsu Homma
    Norman I. Hirose
    Shizuko "Susie" Sakai
    Tom Akashi
    Yasu Koyamatsu
Source: Densho Digital Archives

Robert Oppenheimer (1904–1967), physicist,
and Álvar Núñez Cabeza de Vaca (1490–1558), explorer

Still Life with Conquerors: Oppenheimer at the Window, de Vaca in the Tub

Pasó por aquí…

holding tank motel room
never knew containment more bare
three beauty marks flash-fused,
door, bed, plate-glass pinning desert,
non-smoking so I snuck Marlboros in
under my tongue, I made the sky cringe cadmium red
unflattered the aftermath with cigarette burns on the duvet
a division of light, a demarcation of then and from now on
found myself trace remainders contaminating
security chains, revenant conversations, stucco,
the ghosts of devolving trysts,
strangers' lungs revolting against
a silence that lingers even after the maids
…

Gideon murmured ligaments to life
in drawer piled with skins so fresh
each witch-dog haunting the parking lot converted,
de Vaca and his tamemes in the bathroom
swaddled conquest in soaked hand towels
drowned it like an unwanted brood
I have passed here too but never left
fed on the view, the bitumen bubbling-up fountains
of youth at noon, cauliflower clouds each dusk,
bulbs chanting, burning-out, cars howling romantic anonymities,
highway pandemonium staining
carpet, pillow, coffee pot, tub, a palimpsest,
stratigraphy we crossed, recrossed, crossed-out
I am becoming the life my pacing rubs out of this thin rug

...
passage ritualized binding, trust wadded
like gum on the desk's underbelly jammed beneath
the window where New Mexico bruised
the color of a fermented sun, out here we burn our dead
or atomize them into history or decant new spirits out of old,
new scars mounded upward
womb-clouds, mushroom blasts, countdowns,
slip on dimestore shades, lick finger, test the downwind
de Vaca loading up his Trans Am getting the hell out of range,
settle back, drown scotch in water in the ice bucket,
burn down to the filter, toast the dead,
split curtains like a flayed god,
wave at the tamemes reclining by the poolside
bathers resting as Cézanne swaps hues
pray you don't get retinal cancer from all this witness
from here on out measure the horizon
by how blind the blast leaves us
Yes, said the countdown,
Yes, the neighbors' headboard slamming,
Yes, the tailpipes screaming,
and now I see all we've taken
taking to the hills

C. Samuel Rees

Conquerors compose history and in hindsight are canonized and/or reviled for it. Robert Oppenheimer and Cabeza de Vaca were two such men who imprinted the Southwestern landscape inexorably with their passage. What sort of regrets might each have when, decades or centuries later, they find themselves still haunting the land they changed?

Pasó por aquí: I passed through here; tamemes: porters

Tom C. Lea III (1907–2001), muralist/artist

Lonely Town

We drank tea together, went to dinner at Cottage Grove Avenue
afterward. We eloped and your mother hated it; your father,
the reprobate, didn't give a damn. El Paso was no East Coast
Terre Haute, Indiana, but my folks wanted to meet you.
I look back at these moments, admitting I'd rather blank them out,

leave the key in the door at the house in Santa Fe, lock it all up,
walk away from your memory. I don't like talking about it. Thinking
about it. That was in April. Granny went next in June, then Mother
in December. It reminded me of the storms we saw in the distance,

across in Mexico, how they seemed far away — small, harmless.
Then there was thunder, lightning, rain, wind. I saw all of them together
in one body, looking at the sky, the gray against the red and pale blues
of the desert. Gnarled branches without leaves or green — a solitary
      woman,
scarf trailing behind her. Acequia trees, a lonely town on the border.

Rachel Anna Neff

Tom C. Lea III was an artist, illustrator, muralist, novelist, and war correspondent. His paintings capture the essence of the Southwest and his World War II painting That 2,000 Yard Stare *defined the phrase "thousand yard stare" in English lexicon. The painting* Lonely Town *was created shortly after 1936 — what Lea called "a strange year" because he lost three of the most important women in his life — his first wife, Nancy, his grandmother, and then his mother.*

Constellation

I raised my pincers and undulated
toward her. I tell you,
she moved fast out that door
and I followed her into the night

sky. She can't escape me. I twinkle
from the nether regions
and watch her run. What is she
afraid of? She's the one who

startled me and chased me
into the southern sky to protect
myself by Antares' side. Up here my
black eyes interblend; besides

I'm too old to do any chasing
and will remain snuggled among
the others. But I'd rather be down
there scuttling across the sand.

Gayle Lauradunn

The scorpion comes in many forms: the nocturnal venomous arachnid of which there are about 800 species; the desert dweller that people run from; and the eighth sign of the zodiac (in Greek legend Scorpio stung Orion to death).

John Gaw Meem IV (1894–1983), architect

Legacies

August 7, 1945, Santa Fe

Alice, dear,

A stumbling rummage through nightfall's shade
unearthed this old picture, and the *CRACK!*
of a mallet strike resounded through my head
wood on hard wood falling . . . rolling. . . .

I often conjure our uncommon colleagues,
creative Brahmins, hackers all. We smacked cordial
cannon shots under noon-day suns, no dapple,
heads down, so secure in our singularity

nothing more right then than croquet and yearnings
to scratch new tracks in the sand. We ignored
our mutual illness, dreamed over raw eggs, gamed,
bowed to enforced rest, content in the coddling.

We lacked for nothing, took advantage, pushed out
phlegm, raised knees higher, stretched strides, moved on
up. And up! You wring words, I design, Carlos paints.
Bill heals, Katherine flies. She *flies*, Alice!

But in this murk of night I dredge up Dorothy
spitting and flittering and fawning over all manner
of men. That turncoat up on the Hill funnels her needs
into coddling clandestines, plays blindfold nurse

to Kali, eats fat secrets, spews out comfort and ease,
quiets clattering skulls. And now have you heard,
Alice, of yesterday's unspeakable trespass,
our fierce ruinous rain? Father & Trinity & Sons

now Holy Ghosts blistered and burning, stark shadows
fission-fused into building shards and buckled sidewalks,
flat immutable monuments to madness. Did we grind
through cures and comebacks for worlds cracked wide?

Have you words for this, Alice? Surely we recoil in accord.
To you, dear friend, I admit I blubber and howl, enraged
beyond understanding. My bowels twist hard sour.
Shame and hate clabber my marrow. I can't locate myself.

It's all out of whack, Alice, fractured. Can't sleep. . . .
Never you mind, dearest, don't worry.
The picture's yours to keep. . . .
I trust this finds you.

Yours ever truly,

John G. M.

Mikki Aronoff

Architect John Gaw Meem writes to poet Alice Corbin Henderson of his despair over the role Dorothy McKibbin played as gatekeeper for the Manhattan Project and over the U.S. bombing of Hiroshima. All three were graduate "lungers," former residents of Sunmount TB Sanatorium in New Mexico.

Edna Gladney (1886–1961), children's rights campaigner

That Gladney Woman

I learned the label early on, *Bastard*,
remember playground taunts,
new friends snatched away. But life changed
when I was sent to Dallas at eighteen;
I met Sam. He was already twenty-eight,
but it was a love match. Ten joyous years we shared,
though on our Cuban honeymoon
I lost our only child — a tubal pregnancy
that rendered me sterile. How could I not
take up children's causes?

*There are no illegitimate children,
only illegitimate parents*, was my rallying cry,
I had the stigma of the *Illegitimate* stamp
eliminated from Texas birth certificates,
then pressed on to win adoptees
the same inheritance rights as natural children.
I preened each time the legislature cursed me
That Gladney Woman.

I pushed hard for the purchase
of West Texas Maternity Hospital.
There we gave our young women hospital names,
for confidentiality, and staff provided both care
and training for them. I glowed
when the board renamed it the Edna Gladney Home.
My one-year stint as Superintendent
stretched into thirty-three.

I have to grin, complacent, when I reflect
on 10,000 adoptions, racial considerations ignored.
I was a very liberal woman for my time.
Just think, 10,000 children saved,
and I dressed every one,

presented him to his new parents,
kept in touch with many
by letter or telephone for years. Not a bad life's work
for a little bastard from Milwaukee.

Ann Howells

Edna Gladney is best known today for her leadership role in establishing and running the Edna Gladney Home. Unmarried women were given pre-natal care, and adoption arrangements were made for their babies. In 1941, MGM made a movie of her life, Blossoms in the Dust, *starring Greer Garson, but Gladney found the fictionalization of her life so distasteful that she privately referred to the movie as "Buds in the Dirt."*

J. Frank Dobie (1888–1964), writer and folklorist

A Piece of My Mind

Looks like I've pissed 'em off again!
The Board of Regents ordered me to keep
an office on campus, so I dragged an old desk
down to the boiler room and posted a sign:

> *J. Frank Dobie, Professor of English*
> *Office Hours: Damn Seldom!*

Don't know why folks make such a fuss.
I'm just a writer who loves life and times
of the old Southwest. Do they put me
on a pedestal because I speak my mind,
poke fun at bigotry? I'd rather be independent
and starve than thrive on conformity!
I'm not starving, if you haven't noticed.

I'm a proud liberal Democrat. I'm not afraid
to speak up for Labor or take a stand for civil rights.
Any fool knows we *MUST* integrate this university!
To fire our president and liberal professors proves
these Regents' minds have finally petrified
and need no longer be counted among the living.
Homemade American fascism can take an example
from the state capital of Texas!

Other universities leaped at the chance to have me
chair their English departments. Why raise a ruckus
over me not having a doctorate? Everyone knows
my opinion on the average PhD thesis: *Nothing more
than transferring bones from one graveyard to another.*
Put that in your pipe and smoke it, Coke Stevenson!

    Travis Blair

―――――――――――

J. Frank Dobie, legendary American folklorist, writer, newspaper columnist, and professor, was known for his outspoken liberal views against Texas state politics — which got him dismissed from the University of Texas faculty at the insistence of Governor Coke Stevenson. However, Lyndon Johnson later awarded Dobie the Medal of Freedom, the highest honor that can be awarded to an American civilian.

Tejano guitarist (circa 1940–1950s)

El Guitarrista

Tu papá wants me to teach you la guitarra. Sí, Mi'jo, he asked me.
Bueno, it'll be easy. A few simple chords for los corridos,
de la gente. Mi guitarra has six strings, but en el tiempo
de mis abuelos, they played el bajo sexto, with six double strings.
Vamos a empezar con "Kiansis," sung in mi familia since the 1860s,
the oldest corrido completo de los vaqueros on the early cattle drives.

*... Esos cinco mexicanos / al momento los echaron, /
y los treinta americanos / se quedaron azorados ...*

¿Mi'jo, no sabes que los gringo cowboys learned from the vaqueros?
Ah, que lástima. . . . I'll also teach you corridos de los hombres
who stood up to los rinches — the Texas Rangers. They killed our
    gente
on puro suspecho, for nothing — we were just Mexicanos to them.
We ended up working the same fields we once owned.

I'll teach you a little today, pero primero necesito un cigarillo.
Give me that white pouch over there y los papelitos también.
I make my own: hold one thin papelito between my fingers,
a line of tobacco, lick it, seal it ... then lick the end.
Pero I don't want you smokin', Mi'jo. I used to be really good.
Ahora mi voz es como un cigarillo burning out; mis dedos,
like gnawed bones.

Ah, now back to la guitarra. Put your fingers on the strings
like this. . . . Did you know the corridos are old, bien viejos?
Hay muchos tipos that were sung in the fields or when la familia
gathered en casa o fiesta, songs passed down from los abuelos.
Pero los jovenes ya no recuerdan; they forget the old ways.

Ahora, to "El Corrido de Gregorio Cortez." Era muy famoso.
Have you heard of it? Sheriff Morris en Karnes County mató
al hermano de Gregorio for a crime they hadn't committed.
Gregorio killed ese sherife and fled like a jackrabbit on foot
y en caballo. Not wanting to hang from a noose, he hardly slept

for hundreds of miles. Gregorio defended himself con su pistola,
the only way back then. Respecto, Mi'jo, that's what la gente wanted.

... *Decía Gregorio Cortez / con su pistola en la mano: /*
"No siento haberlo matado / lo que siento es mi hermano."

¿Te gustó? I traveled the border and sometimes
up to San Antonio. La gente used to ask for me to sing
en las fiestas, también en las cantinas. Ay, los gritos
I would throw when I was un poco borracho.

¿Ya tienes que irte? Pero, we just got started. Okay, then.
Dios te bendiga, Mi'jito. You can come back anytime.
Soy viejito, but I'll be here — si Dios quiere.

Gloria Amescua

Guitarists on the Southwestern border sang corridos in the oral tradition that captured the emotions and history of their people. Although wide-ranging in theme, most related to historical events. The Gregorio Cortez ballad first appeared between the incident of the shooting and his capture in 1901 and remained popular into the 1940s and 1950s. This Tejano guitarist is passing on the tradition to the next generation. Lyrics from: A Texas-Mexican Cancionero: Folksongs of the Lower Border.

los corridos, de la gente: the folk songs of the people; el bajo sexto: the sixth bass; Vamos a empezar con: We'll start with; Esos cinco mexicanos/al momento los echaron,/ y los treinta americanos/se quedaron azorados: Those five Mexicans/ penned up the steers in a moment/ and the thirty Americans/ were left staring in amazement; no sabes que: don't you know that; puro suspecho: sheer suspicion; pero primero necesito: but first I need; Ahora mi voz es como: Now my voice is like; mis dedos: my fingers; Hay muchos tipos: There are many types; Pero los jovenes ya no recuerdan: But young people don't remember anymore; mató: killed; Decía: Said; la mano: the hand; No siento haberlo matado/lo que siento es mi hermano: I don't regret having killed him/ what I regret is my brother's death; Te gustó?: Do you like that one?; los gritos: the shouts; un poco borracho: a little drunk; Ya tienes que irte?: You have to go already?; Dios te bendiga, Mi'jito: God bless you, Sonny Boy; Soy viejito: I am old; si Dios quiere: God willing

Brushy Bill Roberts/Ollie P. Roberts/Billy the Kid (1859–1952), outlaw

Brushy Bill Roberts' Last Story, 1859–1952

I shouldn't have been in Lincoln County jail anyways. See, Governor Wallace back then wrote me a letter, saying he'd pardon me if I testified against the two boys who murdered Sheriff Bradley for killing Mr. Tunsall. I finally said okay I would, but after the boys was convicted by my words, that rapscallion Wallace went back on his letter and decided to hang me too. Made me so mad I broke jail, shot two deputies (one of 'um was my friend, too) and started for Mexico.

But before I left, I stopped to see my Sweetie in Ft. Sumner. I had a friend Pete Maxwell there and wasn't scared even though Pat Garrett was the law. He was telling everybody he was gonna kill me for sure but we were friends back before he got a badge so I didn't take him too serious.

One night, I finally decided to leave. I was telling Sweetie goodbye when Billy Barlow said he was going over to Pete's house real quick for some grub for traveling. He didn't even put his boots on. A few minutes later I heard some banging and two loud shots. I went to the door and heard men yelling, "Sheriff Garrett shot Billy the Kid!" Well, I didn't wait around to put them right! Just jumped my horse and took off. I wasn't dead back in 1881, no sir.

I've gone by many names, but I've been Ollie P. Roberts for a good while here in Hico. Most folks 'round here call me 'Brushy Bill' and that'll probably be my last name. I've been feeling poorly since we got back from askin' for a pardon in New Mexico last week. Governor Mabry and his people in Sante Fe ask me a bunch of mean questions and I got real nervous, so I messed up. Couldn't even remember all the men I killed. Just thinking of it, my heart gallops and my breath kinda stops. I was scared because New Mexico still wants to hang Billy Bonney for killing two deputies when he broke jail over in Lincoln County.

But it'll soon be 1953 and now I'm old, too old to try for another pardon.

I guess that's the end of that.

Barbara Randals Gregg

Brushy Bill Roberts was one of twenty-six different people who claimed at one time or another to be the real Billy the Kid, but he's probably the best known. Several books have been written about him and the evidence that he is the Kid, including several by people associated with the 1952 attempt to get a pardon that had been promised him by New Mexico Territory Governor Lew Wallace in 1881. Brushy Bill became very confused during the interview in November 1952 and possibly had a slight stroke. Walking to the Hico, Texas, post office on December 27, 1952, he died of a massive stroke, the truth of his past still in question.

Mary Colter (1869–1958), architect

Into Dawn's Pink Snow

Mary Colter reminisces on La Posada, Santa Fe, 1958

The Wall Street Journal says my masterpiece
is up for sale. Hand-crafted furnishings
and décor to be auctioned off. Perhaps
Clark Gable, if he's still alive, will make
a winning bid, Charles Lindbergh, Howard Hughes —
those pioneers of aviation who
luxuriated in my fantasy,
my rancho grande, my oasis for
turistas riding Harvey trains, like time
machines, to Winslow, Arizona. I
imagined La Posada sprawling out,
constructed slowly over sixty years
to house a don and doña, niños and
nietos, each new wing, each room, each suite
unique in its own objets d'art — antique
imported urns and chests from Mexico,
wrought-iron ashtrays, lamps of hammered tin,
sandblasted dressers, bedposts, and divans —
creating an illusion of the past.
To sense lives lived a century ago
in Arizona Territory — that
was La Posada's great enchantment, first
to sweat in desert heat, then bask in shade
of elm, broad cottonwood, exotic quince
and pomegranate. Guests could stroll among
both cactus and hibiscus. Fountains spilled
on logs of blazing crystals, harvested
from forests turned to stone. The harmony
I'd realized is out of fashion now.
I've lived too long. I roll my metal chair

with practiced quiet — not awakening
my maid — and throw the paper to the hearth.
Bright flames erupt, and lift me till I soar
through shards of dawn's pink snow on Santa Fe.

Marilyn Westfall

Mary Colter (1869–1958) created whimsical yet historically accurate architecture for the Fred Harvey Company and Santa Fe Railroad during the tourist boom of the early twentieth century. Her style was sensitive to Native-American and Hispanic cultural influences, and complemented the Southwestern landscape. Her Hopi House (1905) and Bright Angel Lodge (1935) remain popular destinations at the Grand Canyon, drawing five million visitors annually.

Quilt (circa 1930s–present)

I Guess There Are Worse Things Than Being Turned into Pillows

I was born years ago — all my life, I had their memories — of family or friends who helped create me. I carried pieces of them long after they were gone. Mary Alice, whose sky-blue go-to-meeting dress finally tore along the seam, gave it to make my two center rings. She said, "My Gram got a double wedding ring when she married and we buried her in it. I want to give this one to my son and his girl when they wed in the spring."

Her quilting circle got busy collecting remnants. Got scraps from the Ott twins' outgrown baby blankets — mostly from Jeffery, the colicky one, stains and all. The batting was donated by Liz Wilson since her son was lost in the war, so his homecoming quilt wasn't needed. She was glad it would be used for a wedding quilt. Those Sunday afternoons, they pulled the quilting frame down from the summer bedroom's ceiling, got extra chairs out, made lemonade and tea cakes. Those long afternoons were filled with laughter, sometimes gossip (quietly spoken), snacks and kitchen smells. I was born in the fall and smelled like apple pie when my newly married couple crawled under me on their first night in their own bed — made them feel like their house was already a home, my special gift.

Sometimes during quilting afternoons, little Barbara's Momma let her work stitches around the edges of the double wedding ring. At 7, her stitches weren't even or very straight, and her knots were big old blobs. So after she went outside to play, her Momma took those stitches out and replaced them with her own straight even line. Barbara never knew the difference until her sister Mildred teased her about it. From what I heard, sometimes those sisters were just tacky to each other.

After creation I was treated with the utmost care. All my life, they praised me. "Just beautiful and warm — a comfort in your old age." People would recognize pieces of me from their table cloths, skirts and blouses. Sometimes after food spills or smoky fireplaces, I'd get a bath — not with that old lye soap, either. Gentle soaking with Ivory flakes and pinning on the line to dry.

I'm faded now with small holes and tears. Well, I've been around for four generations but I still sleep with the baby because I'm so soft. Some of the family's grander quilts are put up on the wall to show off. I never was, but I heard the other day I might get turned into pillows to preserve some of the best pieces of me. I guess there are worse things that could happen at the end of a life.

Barbara Randals Gregg

Originally, quilts were made to keep families warm — waste not, want not — recycling before it was even named. But in reality they were one of the only ways many women had to create and be surrounded by their art. The tiniest stitches, straightest lines, and most beautiful colors and designs were admired first and later entered in quilt shows. In fact, today's resurgence among young quilters is fueled primarily by their creative designs — seen as unique art pieces.

Migrant mother (circa 1953)

Sufrimiento: A Migrant Life

Mi esposo y yo venemos de familias con ranchos y dinero. But raising our own large familia has made us poor. Betito still dreams of oro y plata . . . and winning the Publishers Clearing House prize.

Bouncing back and forth across el Rio Grande, our ten were born en dos países. In hard times, Beto had to sell his delivery truck. Hearing cuentos of rich harvest in southern California, we drove day and night packed like desperate jitanos to set new roots in the Coachella valley. In summers, our familia drives farther north to harvest abundant crops, while living in labor camps . . . and still needing to make enough for our rental back home.

Sometimes we lived in long attached aluminum cabins that were like ovens . . . could hear neighbors' private moments through the walls. Sometimes we had a potbelly stove for cooking. Maybe community toilets and showers. Mostly one-room casas. One time, it was a campo of large tents, with an outhouse and outdoor water pumps — we had to pay to use. We hung blankets over twine to make walls for our boys and girls. Once, in a trailer camp, we barely fit in one. Farmers took housing fees from our paychecks.

I wake first to make desayuno and our work tacos. Mis hijos get up in the dark to eat and dress for the fields. Huge loading trocas drive families to and from the strawberry and tomato fields. When we harvest plums, Beto drives us and our cubetas to the orchards to gather the plums off the ground. The adult work is hell on the children, bending for hours under the scorching sun . . . but how else can we make it? "Que Dios nos perdone." Mi esposo drives them hard, rewarding the fastest with a Hostess cake. I look away and pray when he breaks a thin branch off a plum tree to beat the slow-working ones. "¡Trabajen, más rápido! ¡No sean burros!" Beto insists he is making them stronger trabajadores.

In the fall, when harvest is near over, we return to our hometown. Whenever the landlord has raised la renta, Beto must quickly find another home. The children are chapulines hopping from escuela to escuela. Muchas veces, Beto decides we will stay at la pisca past the start of school. Mis pobres hijos must catch up in their books, or fall behind on their dreams. My biggest hope is for my children to gain mejores futuros con la educación. Mejor vida que nosotros. Like Jesucristo, I bear my cross. Sufrimiento is part of life, but heaven will be my reward.

Movida tras movida, we have become nomads. Pero mis antepasados vienen de varios países . . . I come from a long line of wanderers.

Anjela Villarreal Ratliff

This migrant mother's life reflects the harsh living of many who were forced to choose the migrant lifestyle to provide for their families. It was especially hard for migrant mothers to watch their children work the crops, while hoping they might gain better futures through education.

Sufrimiento: Suffering; Mi esposo y yo venemos de familias with ranchos y dinero: My husband and I come from families with ranches and money; oro y plata: gold and silver; en dos países: in two countries; cuentos: stories; jitanos: gypsies; desayuno: breakfast; trocas: trucks; cubetas: buckets/pails; "Que Dios nos perdone": "May God forgive us"; Mi esposo: My husband; Trabajen, más rápido! No sean burros!": "Work faster! Don't be donkeys!"; trabajadores: workers; mejores futuros con la educación: better futures with an education; Mejor vida que nosotros: Better life than ours; chapulines: grasshoppers; escuela: school; Muchas veces: Many times; la pisca: the harvest; Movida tras movida: move after move; Pero mis antepasados vienen de varios países: But my ancestors come from various countries

Vance Hall Kirkland (1904–1981), painter

I Give What Art Demands

Each morning, I slip my body into straps swinging
from my studio's ceiling. One supports my chest,
another spans the waist, a third cradles thighs,
the last lifts ankles into the air. I dangle above
the canvas like a horizontal astronaut
of art, flying in the room's sky, my back
illuminated by the hot suns of studio lights.

I practice the rhythm of suspension. One hand,
fingertips touched to canvas, steadies my pendulum
body. My other hand grasps a wooden dowel dipped
in color to dot a spotted nebula into being. Blood
rushes, blushes, and sings in my hanging head.
Fumes rise from the oil paint, sear my lungs
like exhaled comets. My muscles cramp
as the moon rolls over the skylight, asks
how long an angel can fly obsessed
with beauty and celestial mind.

It's the angle of my body to the art
that reveals the image's truth —
to paint the desert, I lie in the sand;
to paint mountains, I climb their sides.
To paint the distant cosmos, I must lift
from Earth, rise, hover like a star.

    Carolyn A. Dahl

Vance Kirkland, the "Father of Modern Colorado Painting," is best known for his later work of vibrantly colored dot paintings of outer space. However, anyone who visits his studio can't forget the color-encrusted dowels and the four empty straps hanging over the painting table, attesting to the unique horizontal position he imposed on his body to paint a universe his eyes hadn't seen.

Laura Gilpin (1891–1979), photographer

Laura Gilpin Photographs Dennis Hopper

You are a cave, Dennis, under that black hat.
Take it off. Today your eyes are soft
as those of the deer on Taos Mountain,

as tender as apricots from the ancient trees
along the acequia. I am an old woman,
Dennis, I have seen how people dry up

in the desert wind, how their roots
pull loose. They hang squash blossoms
of turquoise and silver around their necks

hoping that will anchor them to the earth.
But you, Dennis, are comet, long-haired
star, and should be photographed

against the broad back of a winter sky
on one of those days when smoke
from the fogón shoots straight up in the air.

You should be photographed riding
whitewater rapids coursing through
black basalt canyons of the Rio Grande.

Today confined to this room I photograph
the landscape of your face. I know light
can illuminate. I know light can eclipse.

    Susan J. Erickson

Laura Gilpin, known for her photographs of Native Americans and Southwestern landscapes, photographed Dennis Hopper for a book titled A Taos Mosaic.

fogón: corner-set fireplace.

Donald Judd (1928–1994), artist

Sitting on a Curb in Marfa, Texas

Donald Judd muses, circa 1971

In the world's great museums,
paintings crowd one another
like sardines in a tin, as if space,
sacred as it is, doesn't matter.
In my daydream, the artillery

once housed in the sheds of the fort
melts into sheets of mill aluminum.
Just outside the sheds, shadowy
phantoms take up residence
in giant, open boxes of concrete.

My mind basks in the glow
of moons, sunlight, sating itself
with yellow grasses, lavender
mountains, and the answered
prayers of rock, dust, fang, thorn.

Sculpture, at long last, dismounts
the useless nag of its pedestal,
mere *object* on hallowed ground,
representing nothing. Color,
in its myriad cathedrals wrought

with perfection, fabrication, concrete,
enamel, copper, Plexiglass, wood
and steel, absent any presence
of an artist, belts out the bleak,
insensate physics of its properties.

Larry D. Thomas

Donald Judd, one of the most significant American artists of the post-war period, moved to Marfa, Texas, in 1971 and maintained residences there and in New York City for the remainder of his life. He purchased numerous properties in Marfa and the surrounding area that are presently owned by the Chinati Foundation.

Georgia O'Keeffe (1887–1986), artist

Essentials

The ruined hacienda finally
became mine, mostly
because I was Stieglitz's widow.
The time was right for purchase;
his death provided
peace,
freedom,
most of all, cash
for a view I painted over and over,
each brushstroke a prayer.
I allowed only local women
to sand, paint, spread paste,
render delicate
tones and textures.

        Oh, my bedroom!
        Its tight corner window
        that aims
        at the twisting road
        past Abiquiu. When I sat up
        in bed, I could see
        for miles, until
        my eyes failed
        near the end. I rose in socks
        on the soft rock floors,
        ran grateful fingers across
        a wall stained taupe —
        the particular shade coveted and
        scraped slowly
        from a rock face that spoke to me
        at Cerro Pedernal.

That one red pillow punctuates
my white-on-white bed.
The color would vibrate
as I wandered the spare kitchen,
breathing deep of dried herbs.

Rows of stainless-steel canisters still
bear my script. The label
on my favorite reads merely, *good tea.*

    Ann Ritter

Northwest of Santa Fe, Abiquiu is the location of the 5,000-square-foot Spanish Colonial house and grounds that were to become O'Keeffe's most beloved home. The place was in ruins when O'Keeffe first saw it, and she attempted to purchase it more than once, finally succeeding in 1945. As the heir of her husband, Alfred Steiglitz, who died in 1946, O'Keeffe was able to use the couple's collective wealth to pay for a loving restoration that took more than four years. Once she took up residence in 1949, O'Keeffe considered the hacienda her permanent residence and spent most of her time there. Macular degeneration increasingly affected O'Keeffe's eyesight for the last two decades of her life. Although she continued to paint and draw as she aged, and to live quite independently, the quantity and quality of light in the Abiquiu home, as well as its colors, textures and surfaces, became of utmost importance to her continued work as an artist. She remained in or near Abiquiu until she was 96 years old, only leaving because of fragile health to return to Santa Fe, where she died in 1986 at age 99. Now open for tours on a limited basis, her home and studio continue to show how O'Keeffe's personal lifestyle reflected her aesthetic.

Georgia O'Keeffe (1887–1986), artist

Georgia O'Keeffe in Old Age

I sit in a dim room, seeking every flicker of light
from a life just past. I cannot see well enough to paint,
so I resort to words, always a poor substitute.
Through the windows of my house, I can still discern
more sky than earth and know I am home to stay.

As a child I heard the land call me —
shifting grass, ripe soil, birdsong in the tops of trees.
In Sun Prairie I began to capture it all on paper.
"Not those," my mother said. "Portraits. There's a living in that!"
But people were not my calling.

Huge blooms opening out, perfect to the last detail —
petunias — ruffled and silken as foam on shores,
irises — black and white curves round a cowl of deep maroon,
calla lilies — soft white folds with a spike of gold at the heart —
these were my loves. They never betrayed me.

In the desert I glimpsed a hidden self
as dry wind healed my lungs in Palo Duro Canyon.
At night a swirl of stars pricked my eyes and the moon whirled.
At last to Abiquiu, untouched, lonely place
where I could spread my arms wide, be all I am,
both dark and light, see myself in twisted rocks,
in hawks and skulls, in sun that set the world afire.

Now I work with clay, fingers molding in the fading light.
I close my eyes to drift on currents of warm air
over sculpted stone and sand.

Even in the dark
my bones still know this land.

Patricia Spears Bigelow

Born in Sun Prairie, Wisconsin, in 1887, Georgia O'Keeffe began drawing as a child and had decided by age 12 that she would be an artist. Her relationship with renowned photographer Alfred Stieglitz fueled her rise to fame. His multiple betrayals led her to pursue her own vision of art and life in New Mexico where she lived until her death in 1986 at the age of 99.

Kay (circa 1990s), from a Robert Earl Keen song

Hello, My Name's Kay

Yes, Mom got drunk, and Dad got drunk
At the Christmas party,
But when Robert Earl wrote that song about them
That's when the hell really started.
Oh, the Aggies sing and he's got fame,
But there I am in another fool drunk's refrain
About the new wife, Kay (that's me), talking all about AA.
Damn you, Robert Earl, you ruined Noël.

Back then, I was barely a member of that clan,
Just been married for a year or so to Ken.
Thank you, Jesus, all his kids are now growed and gone,
And have Christmases of their own to attend.
I can't say nothing bad about them
Because I'd have to begin again with my amends.
Steps eight and nine are a bitch, and so is ten.
Damn those kids, for years they ruined Noël.

> We always fry the turkey;
> The ballgame's always on.
> I drink the Diet Rites until they're all gone.
> Hey now I bought myself a selfie stick.
> Everybody stop and pose real quick.
> Robert Earl, stop doing that.
> Do these jeans make my ass look fat?
> My name's Kay and have you heard of AA?
> Merry Christmas and Happy Holiday.

I'm not sure how Bobby wrote that song.
Most Christmases, he's passed out, sawing logs,
Or telling lies about Willie or Lyle or Sherry hitting the road.
And no, that grouch never drove to no convenience store.
Sister's Mexican boyfriend accepts that chore,
And keeps everybody from getting bored

With booze and smokes and lights and lots of fake snow.
Thank you, my amigo, for saving Noël.

Now here's a secret about me and Ken.
Remember Fred and Rita from Harlingen?
Well we snuck out to the motor home and let ourselves in.
Everybody in that stuck-up town
Must have heard me praising Jesus real loud.
And, oh, those shocks, they were really tight.
In the afterglow, we shared my Marlboro Lights.
Thank you, Ken, that was some Noël.

> The turkey is a carcass,
> Another ballgame's on.
> Smoking Salems since the Marlboros are gone.
> The yard is filled with our pick-up trucks.
> I spend my Christmases with all these drunks,
> But I'll never drink again, I swear to God.
> Hey, everybody, it's Feliz Navidad.
> My name's Kay and I love the double A's,
> Merry Christmas and Happy Holidays.

Lyman Grant

Kay led the anonymous life of a recovering alcoholic until she married into the family of a popular singer-songwriter from Texas. Robert Earl Keen did not tell the full story in his classic song "Merry Christmas from the Family."

Gabrielita Pino (1905–2000), curandera

La Curandera

I. Invocation

Summer rains over Mora Valley have fattened roots,
tinged grasses, made them ready for tinctures and oils;
the gods have danced in petals and leaves are now ready for infusions.

O, Mother of God, guide my steps on this 12th day of August.
Anchor my body in this generous tierra, my spirit in your holy embrace
as my hands gather and pluck this summer's windfall.
Press Your light into petals of malvas, baptize alhucemas with Your
      fragrance;
gather Your grace into inmortal, oils of ruda and punche mexicano.

II. Response

This grinding stone and pestle, gifts from abuela,
served generations of curanderas before me;
their wisdom has entered my hands, fingers,
even the sinews of my flesh and bone.
With Your grace I, too, have become a sabia.

Guide me as I treat mal de aire lodged beneath hardened brows,
dose open wounds and ulcers with añil del muerto.
Bless the cota to relieve kidney problems,
osha to ease stomach cramps; maravilla root for inflamed joints;
altamisa, to treat colds and fevers during winter;
coyaye for baths to relieve arthritis.
Stay by me as I rid spirits of sustos and the mal de ojo.

Soon Euphonia will give light to my grandchild,
and I am called to be her partera.
O God lend my hands to Your service;
press Your strength into oils of inmortal to stretch her flesh,

open her womb, ease the passage of new life into daylight.
Bless the alhucema teas to soothe her cries of pain,
malvas to free her afterbirth, coyaye to cleanse her
and keep ready to relieve her baby's colic.
Soon I will pass on my wisdom to my granddaughter.
I pray she can carry on my trade.

III. Benediction

My baskets are now empty of summer's bounty,
dried petals of altamisa locked in their weave.
My potions are stored in jars, in packets, on shelves
ready to shrug off the hoary breath of winter's ills.
Gabrielita has been brought to light, and
the last days of summer gild her cheeks with health;
her eyes are deep with promise of carrying on after me
when I answer the final call to move across the veil.
The gift of healing has been a gift of grace from You, O Lord,
the touch of my hands has carried Your pulse:
Gracias, Dios Mío.

Paula Miller

Curanderismo in Northern New Mexico came from Mexico with Spanish Colonialism. In 1997, at age 91, Gabrielita of Buena Vista was still practicing as a yerbera (herbalist), sobadora (folk chiropractor) and partera (midwife). Anselmo F. Arellano of the University of New Mexico interviewed Gabrielita of Buena Vista for the March/April 1997 issue of Mother Earth Living. *This poem is based on his article.*

malvas: mallow; alhucemas: lavender; inmortal: antelope horns; ruda: rue; punche mexicano: native tobacco; sabia: wise one; mal de aire: bad air; añil del muerto: gold weed; cota: Hopi tea; osha: wild lovage; maravilla: wild four o'clock; altamisa: mountain mugwort; coyaye: snake broom; sustos: frights; mal de ojo: evil eye; partera: midwife

Jim Corbett (1933–2001), activist, environmentalist

Corbett's Conatus

> *When the wind wails a dirge and snow sifts in rivulets through the sagebrush, I've hugged the sticky-pink, death-chilled body of a newborn lamb under my coat, and its heart fluttered in reply.*
> ~ *Jim Corbett*

Though fingers and toes gnarled, folding over each other,
I clenched my staff tap, tap, tapping, poking parched sands
of Sonora's desert lands — saguaro-juniper, mesquite, ocotillo,
yucca, cat-claw. . . . Eremite seeking sacred life and peace,
I trekked rock-rugged terrain, climbing craggy canyons
and hidden dreams.

Some folks called my late life "cowbalah,"
for I'd fused a fractured Judaic and Quaker doctrine,
consistent with Spinoza's conatus, *Nature's law*,
Life's will to persist.
True, I did walk and talk to cows amid mystic canyons.
And when cows were old and done with scant-grass grazing,
done with pulling old posts, deep roots, and heavy loads,
I killed them and ate them.
And yes, I did kill and eat old Stripe, my favorite bull,
whom I'd led and fed as friend, and when he was done
with striving and blessing, I ate him in *Allegiance*
to the Peaceable Kingdom of our co-creative communion.
"How can you eat what you've loved?" you ask.
I answer: *I avoid eating anyone*
I haven't known and cherished.

In a time before cow time, I walked goats for my soul.
I drank their milk and foraged desert greens and seeds.
Then I met a refugee fleeing death from Central America,
fleeing arrest, degradation, and deportation from my America.
Later, I donned black as Padre Jaime and I crossed borders

past Nogales to El Santuario de Nuestra Señora de Guadalupe
to rescue Guatemalans, Nicaraguans, Salvadorans seeking asylum.
Old goat herder herding, I escaped attention, suspicion:
You know how it is with Power; He ignores the Humble.
We ushered nearly a million folks in an over-ground sanctuary
before we were discovered, arrested, indicted.
I said *We will not cease.* . . . And we didn't.

Aging hermit, semi-exiled, I walked Cascabel's wild,
and I saw *God in every other*, whether mesquite or man,
mountain lion or calf, coyote or cactus. Time fused.
And *on a desert mountain, amidst the hush of soaring granite*
in a time before this time, I learned that to *open
a forgotten spring . . . long ago gone dry, to know of a place
where a juniper is a nurse tree for a Saguaro*
is to know sacred conatus, to see *God in every other*,
to feel life rivulet in a heart's flutter.

Charlotte Renk

Conatus *is Spinoza's term for the will of a being to live. Italicized phrases are taken from* Goatwalking *and* Sanctuary for All Life: The Cowbalah of Jim Corbett. *Corbett was a political activist, co-founder of sanctuary movement, a "cowman" and "practical mystic," who dedicated his semi-exiled life to "earth rights" as he walked Sonoran wildlands around Cascabel, Arizona, with refugees, goats, and cows. Mentor to my son, Corbett introduced us to Stripe, his favorite bull on one of his latter-day walks.*

Thomas Elwin Castello (circa 1940–1990), security officer, alien theorist

The Archuleta Whistleblower

My name is Thomas Elwin   Castello. I was the Senior
Security Technician   at the base below this mesa

of elevated strangeness near   Dulce, New Mexico where
a 1960s think tank developed   a mole machine that melted

rock using nuclear-powered,   wolfram graphite-tipped
drill cones which located   the original ice caves

and sulfur springs that   aliens found perfect
especially the finished walls   polished smooth as black

glass. Dungeons & Dragons   fanatics
and other human workers   have been the biggest

problem wandering the   Off Limits area,
bottomless shafts wide   enough to drive

a semi-truck through   rooms emanating
a greenish phosphorescent   glow

where lizard people   thrived in the labyrinths.
I knew of disabled   video cameras,

altered cow blood, and   smuggled documents
concerning the copper and   molybdenum. I speak out

only now, under penalty   of death, because I learned
of an inmate with high   sperm count ready to escape

rather than lose his soul   before creating another
non-gender bio-form.   I knew this was not

the usual hospital security   job. I'm telling the truth—
I once protected   research for marvelous new cures

on the surface of Earth.   If you don't believe me,
ask the Apaches, or see   the mutilated animals,

or touch the autumn joy   that survive desert heat
with their fleshy leaves   and scalloped margins.

John Milkereit

In 1961, Castello was a young sergeant stationed at Nellis Air Force Base who was a military photographer with top secret clearance. He eventually left the Air Force in 1971 and worked for the RAND Corporation where his security clearance was eventually upgraded to ULTRA-7. He eventually married and had a son, but Castello is currently presumed either dead or missing. My guess is that Mr Castello is the product of someone's vivid imagination.

Stephanie Lynn "Stevie" Nicks (1948–), singer/songwriter

Granddaddy Jess

Four years old, I balanced
on that bar top — my first stage —
speckled with the shine of new quarters
the regulars tossed at my feet.
Some day it'd be roses and baby's breath
cushioning the path of my platforms
(six- or eight-inch heels) elevating me
as Granddaddy's hands had
lifting me up to that bar.
My Granddaddy,
a country-western singer
who never really made it
beyond the saloon circuit
of smaller Southwestern cities,
always said or sang or scolded,
"Sing like you mean it, Stevie!
Like you mean it."

Today sequins, rhinestones, silvery threads
in brocaded chiffons shipped from India.
And the sweat-and-tear gloss
that could come only from a song
sung with meaning, sung with urgency,
to please a disappointed Granddaddy
so he might see beyond his failures
to the child still bowing there
in a glittering shower of coins.

Michael Montlack

The speaker Stevie Nicks was born in Phoenix. Growing up she also lived in Albuquerque, El Paso, Salt Lake City, and Los Angeles. Her grandfather Jess (Aaron Jess Nicks) performed in small venues in the Southwest, bringing little Stevie along. As an adult, Stevie returned to Arizona to live in Scottsdale.

The 21st Century (2000–present)

Judy Ann Magers (1942–2007), burro rider

La Reina

I take no charity. I shun your pity.
I am not homeless.
My hat makes a fine roof,
My colorful blankets are my floor.
My fragrance, the smell of creosote bush.

My journey follows the bar ditch,
My rhythm, the flop of my burro's ears,
My music, the clop of his hooves.
And I'm proud to ride tall,
My spurs and boots part of me.

No tent, no fire, I trade comfort for independence.
And I don't want to talk,
For I am full with thousands of sunsets,
And billions of stars,
In a quiet so still, I hear my heart beat.

Do not lay your story over mine.
I have my secrets. Not lonely, just alone.
Answering only to my burro and myself,
I ask your respect.
For I am La Reina: Queen of her own life.

Lucy Griffith

Judy Magers, nicknamed "The Burro Lady" or "La Reina," wandered the roads of far West Texas for thirty years riding her burro. Her legal address was: On the Land, Terlingua, Texas. She died of natural causes on January 26, 2007.

Sid Goodloe (1930–), rancher

Sweetie

The spike buck raised its head, then ducked.
I hit the doe instead. As I dressed her out, her belly
thumped under old coyote scars — they always
go for the softest part of their kill. I slit her open
gently and pulled out a kicking fawn, twirled it
round and round by its legs until the birth-juice
flew out of the lungs, off its long, blue tongue.
Wrapped in a horse blanket, it shivered, watched
me with eyes wet as gully washers as I loaded
the body of its mother into the truck. Wasn't
nothing to do but take them both home.

I called her Sweetie — she being a girl and all,
and liking sugar in her milk. I made a bottle
from a rubber glove, and she ate right well,
shooting up to the size of a calf. Frisky too.
She followed me to the arroyo, chased jack-
rabbits around the petroglyphs with
the dogs, nudged my face every time
I bent over anthills to search their
mounds of sand for Indian beads
they always bring to the surface.

When I went to town for supplies, Sweetie
rode in the pickup cab, head out the window
with the dogs. *Growing your own venison,
Sid?* the store clerks cracked. *When's supper?*
Or, *You look like hell, Sid. New girlfriend
keeping you up all night?* Since Sweetie
came, I don't get a lick of sleep. When
the dogs sound off at night, I jump up
with my gun, fearing coyotes got ahold
of her. Tomorrow, I'm making her a bed
in the kitchen on ma's old quilt so I get

some shut-eye. Yesterday, I worried
myself to the bottom of a whiskey bottle
fearing she would run off and get herself shot.
Today, I made her a necklace from Indian
beads to mark her as a pet, not meat. Sure
as hell wish that spike buck hadn't ducked.

Carolyn A. Dahl

Sid Goodloe is a passionate, outspoken New Mexico rancher who dislikes Smokey the Bear for discouraging forest fires in a climate where nothing rots to feed the soil. He has spent a lifetime restoring the watersheds and grasslands of his Carrizo Valley ranch and teaching others to become responsible caretakers for the animals and the land on which they live. He always intended to write his own book, but became instead a beloved character in others' writings.

Carlos Cortés (1958–), faux bois artist

Tree

I built this tree
>steel girders, mesh and concrete
>and worked the concrete with
>forks and spoons and pigments,
>my secret mix,
>to give the tree
>believable bark

to the eye and to the hand.

I spent some years resisting learning,
refusing tradition,
afraid to fall into that trap, but now

my hands are sure, I've come to love
the family art form passed down
into my hands, this forest alchemy.

The metalworkers
built a staircase that spirals
around the trunk, up to a nest
to watch from,

and at the roots I built
a cave space,
a place to sit, read stories, play.

If you look closely, in the half-dark
of the root cave,
look with your eyes *and* with your hands.
You'll find —

scraped into the surface of the concrete —
my children's names,

this tradition
passed along —

this tree, family.

    Jim LaVilla-Havelin

This poem is in the voice of Carlos Cortés, faux bois sculptor, who learned the folk art sculpture medium from his family, and who built the tree that stood in the entry lobby of the San Antonio Children's Museum on Houston Street, as well as pieces on the Riverwalk's Museum Reach.

Helen Ruth Jones (1921–), grandmother

Homing

Where I stand, stood
a two-room school, of sorts.
A road right there that cut
to a church. Another
that stopped at my family's
milk-wash door. I'm pretty
sure the P.O. was on
a corner here, *or was it
there?,* where now lies
a rogue cotton boll, blown
over from Homer Hitt's
big field. It's been so long,
but I hear them all
yelling, my ten brothers
and sisters, fighting over
the one dog in town, the one
I hid in the trunk back
in Texas. Apart from thirst,
he survived the five
hundred miles happy. Better
than my mother, who
never quit crying: too many
coyotes, no roses, and no
friend to help mend skirts
ripped by prickly pear
and caliche. But this is where
I learned to rassle with the best
of the boys and where I first
touched my husband.
I can't recall when everyone
fled, or why. It wasn't
so bad. I would've stayed
had my baby not come
so soon and my father not

coaxed us all again
to another naked place.
My great-niece guides me
to my Buick and guesses
which pasture leads back
to asphalt. At home,
she'll look it up: *Richland*
Best Time To Visit:
Any time. Remains:
Nothing. And we'll rest
on the porch and watch
the bobwhite lure
his mate to bed,
a shy whistle.

Melissa Jones Brewer

Helen Ruth Jones and her family moved from East Texas to the small town of Richland, NM, in 1936. She was second oldest in her family and was fourteen when they moved to Richland. She recently returned to the old Richland homestead to find the entire town gone. Helen is my grandmother.

Lynda Lanker (1943–), portrait artist

Tough by Nature

Shading her tanned face with the brim of a felt hat
and to an audience of heifers and her favorite horse,
she breaks into a smile —
but not because my camera demands it . . .
the answer to that prompt would be,
just take the damned picture.
Instead, I let the lens catch her natural gaze
as she assesses another ranch day done, the sun
cooling in the west as she sets herself down
on the raw plank porch she built herself
the last year she had something to prove.
I use its cedar posts to frame the shot,
let her carpentry begin to tell the story
she has written with her sweat.
The months spent alone.
The money made and gone.
Wanting one more angle, I zoom in
to study the map of her furrowed skin,
choose a close-up of her eyes to become
the biography of what she has just told me:
that through everything that has been
born and broke and branded and buried,
she has held her ground, faced the wolves head-on
and had faith in the land and the hands
that work it, knowing most times there is no need
to worry — this old world and the brave women
in it recreate themselves in all their glory
every splendid morning, every starlit evening,
every time a man sets posts on how things have to be.

    Anne McCrady

Here, accomplished portrait artist Lynda Lanker takes a photograph of her subject. This poem borrows the title of the traveling collection and hardcover book of Lanker's stunningly lifelike depictions of western women and their disappearing lifestyle — Tough by Nature: Portraits of Cowgirls and Ranch Women of the American West.

Candy Barr/Juanita Dale Slusher (1935–2005), stripper, dancer

Juanita Dale Slusher Meets St. Peter

You do know me — right?
I'm not just Nita, well now I am. I used to be Candy Barr.
I saw that look — as I recall, you weren't always a saint.
So where was He when I was wearing cowboy boots and not much else?

All the men loved me, but I was a just a teenager.
You men were like dogs — panting after a treat or the kill.
I guess I wasn't much better, but I was young, and I loved to dance.
After a while I realized it was a pretty easy life for the 1950s.
I left Big D for Vegas and LA, made a pile of money and accumulated
generous friends — by the way, where did Mickey Cohen and Jack Ruby end up?
They were good to me — heck, Jack even gave me some of his dachshunds.
Oh, confidential? Hmmm.
What about John Connally? He should be in heaven just for my pardon.
Right — confidential, I know.

Funny, that's the thing, there was nothing confidential in my life.
I had this naïve idea that I would marry a man, have children

turn into Harriet Nelson and everyone would love me.
That's really what I wanted: friends, family who loved me.
In the end, I got most of it; did you know I'm a grandma? Texas took me back.

But now here I am, being judged by a man who left his job and wife
to go tell other people how to live their lives.
Sometimes I think God must have the best sense of humor!
So what's it going to be? Heaven or hell — I've never been good at waiting.

Adamarie Fuller

Nita Slusher was the famous stripper Candy Barr, who performed in Dallas and across the Southwest in the '50s and '60s. She also made one of the first 8mm "blue movies." Candy had many male friends from all walks of life and was interviewed frequently by the FBI. She died at seventy in Edna, Texas.

Brian Joseph Chavez (1973–), Cochiti mercy-killer

Milky Way

One winter night when I was four years old, icy roads and too much alcohol pushed my parents to the other side. My grandmother stepped up to care for me. She gave me my language and taught me how to become a human being. She took me to live with her in a small Indian pueblo along the Rio Grande. We grew to love each other and came to depend on each other. We needed each other for our hearts to be full.

Now, at 97, blind and unable to walk, the old woman begs to die. "Shoot me."

I turn away. "I cannot take your life, you are my own flesh and blood."

"But there is no taking. I give it to you. If you love me, you will put me to rest."

A 12-gauge shotgun rests behind the door of our little adobe house. It is hunting season. I want an elk or at least a deer. We need meat for winter. I will go into the woods and leave her. She will die, I tell myself. But how cruel to let her die alone.

I stay.

The floor creaks beneath me as I walk to the room where my grandmother sleeps. Her cot is pushed under a window so she can watch the night sky. Looking at the Milky Way she has told me: "This is where we go when we leave." Asleep, she looks so peaceful. I cock the trigger, close my eyes, and silence the drumbeat of her heart.

Barbara Robidoux

This poem is based on an event that occurred when a Cochiti tribal member of a New Mexico pueblo shot and killed his grandmother at her request. Subsequently, he was arrested and tried for first degree murder; for this mercy-killing the perpetrator has received a sentence of twenty-five years in jail.

Wolf (circa 2000–), Cochiti boy

They Named Me Wolf

I see ancient dancers come from aspen groves,
mark time with their feet's tiny bells.
It is the holy season when they dress
with the river's gifts — turtle shells, feathers.

Soon I, too, will paint my chest sky-blue,
yarrow-yellow, pine-green. Hours of chant,
our drummers call eagle, fox, parrot spirits.
In spring I go with the men into corn fields

below ochre-red buttes to dig out acequias until the river
rushes a flood of star-flecked waters into ditches.
I speak for this river carrying the stillborn, the dying —
this water that quenches thirst of bosque, merganzers,

warblers and ash-throated flycatchers.
And if the Sacred is a river cluttered
with rusted batteries, tires, paint cans,
bones of horses, oil, solvent, plastic bottles?

She rides on, cagey in her silence,
faithful as the wolf, as betrayed.
Here on the Otowi bridge, I watch
the river slip into darkness, its skin of stars.

   Renny Golden

Wolf is the name of a Cochiti Pueblo boy who is the son of a friend. He has just begun to take part in the sacred dances which allow him an expressive outlet. His silence holds a longing and a history.

Rebecca "Becky" Smith (1931–), rancher

Becky of the B-C Ranch

He left me this ranch, and I miss him, I do.
He taught me so much; when he gave me this ranch
it was such a surprise I thought I'd dance all the way
through the canyon! He handed his last round-up over to me.
I found my place when I came to work for him all those years ago,
Oklahoma, Alabama, long gone forgotten.
I guess that doesn't matter too much to you,
Sweet Red, but it should. On my watch first thing
we did was to get rid of the cowboys,
didn't we? We didn't need the men,
they never listen to a woman boss anyway.
Those boys on the ranch were a hardheaded
tobacco spitting waste of time. Women are gentle mostly, but
I'd sooner hit a cowboy in the head with a 2x4
than let them hit you, and I wouldn't blink an eye
showing them how a cattle prod could be used,
before I'd let them use one on you.

Sweet Red, queen of cattle, I learned how to choose your bulls,
learned you give birth not much different
than women do. Your cries beat out the coyote racket
those long midnights we shared under cold-shouldered moons
waiting for your babes. I had to turn a hard deaf ear
to your heartbroken calls when round-up time
took your calves away. Better you were not sentient
(no matter what they told me in veterinary school).
I know you feel, I know your heart.
Better I were not sentimental, but seems I am
so much moreso these breathless days.
My heart beats too fast, they tell me.

This fence that separates you and me
is only going to get bigger and harder to cross.
These days I watch you from the window

more often than I walk up to you, but I am still here,
Sweet Red, still here, remembering how I
rode for years fighting that wind that blows
across this valley until we traded the horses for Kubotas.
Guess it's not too dang romantic, but we went with
whatever worked best to keep going, we had to.
That pesky prevailing breeze that worries the trees
and makes patterns in your hair has blown all this time,
but we are still here, stood our ground, our roots have held.

I have lapped up the scent of the rain-soaked creosote
like it was honey, gazed at cat claw blossoms dripping dew
and smelled snow before it came over the mountain.
I broke ice in the water troughs and built a fire to warm the cats,
chased off a drunken yahoo aiming a shotgun at my quail,
drove to God-awful Odessa to get supplies when I was forced to.
I breathed a whole lot easier when Ft. Stockton was in the rear mirror
and the blue vistas, Mitre Peak, and the Twin Sisters came into view.
I never wanted to leave here, not for an hour, why would anyone want to?
When I had to go away, Sweet Red, I always hurried home.

Darla McBryde

In 1970, Becky Smith came to work for Perry Cartwright, owner of the B-C Ranch in Alpine, TX. Mr. Cartwright was 91 when he died in 1981 after first giving Smith the ranch. Smith has run the ranch as mostly an all-woman outfit, because the women were of like minds in regards to how the cattle should be treated. She is 85, and still actively involved with the B-C.

Marvin L. Dorsey (1966–), rancher

Eulogy in Lancaster

Despite the heat all the animals are standing.
In these temperatures they should be low,

close to the ground — llamas, goats, a team of ducks,
a rooster, his harem, a couple of geese,

a pig named Barbeque. They seem to know
the backhoe is not here to build a road,

prepare the foundation for a shed
or a barn, nor to move boulders

or to lay cable in the California outback.
They seem to know the old horse is gone.

The corral is quiet and still,
the wind is what now kicks up dirt.

Missing is the horse's whinny, the shake
of his crest, the sharp slap of his tail thrashing flies.

The backhoe's big engine
competes with the growl of thunder.

I wait until the horse is lowered in the hole,
piles of churned soil scooped back into place.

I pay the driver cash. He rumbles his truck
home at dusk, down the long desert road,

leaving the landscape undisturbed but for thick
tire treads and a dark mound in the back acre.

No time to watch the sun set behind storm clouds,
for the yard must be secured, the animals fed.

Outside the tall chain fence roam coyote, and hawk,
rattlesnake, tumbleweeds — the great Milky Way.

Tomorrow I'll clean the stall and tack and feed bins.
Tomorrow I'll mark the grave with a circle of stones.

Mary Torregrossa

The poem was written when poet and friend Marvin L. Dorsey called me on his cell phone to share his experience overseeing the burial of one of his ranch horses as it took place. He was standing outside in the back acre of his desert property in Lancaster, California and talked through his feelings and the events as they happened. As he spoke I started to take notes that I knew later I'd turn into a poem.

Mollie Taylor Stevenson, Jr. (1946–), rancher, cowgirl

Rising Song

Some ask how a woman like me,
college-educated and a successful model,
can turn away from city life
for the tough work of Texas ranching.

I always say, "It has to be in your blood."
Seven generations of my family have lived here,
starting with E. R. Taylor, white son of a slave owner
who purchased great-grandmother
Ann George in 1856.

A strong woman who nursed great-grandfather
back to health after Vicksburg and tuberculosis,
she lived as his wife, birthing six children.
All graduated from college.

This is their legacy — my life — 640 acres.
Here we roll prairie grass into bales
of sun-baked hay while sweaty horses flip
stiff tails, swat flies, and wait for a good brushing.

During segregation, Mother brought out truckloads
of children, banned from public parks, to play
in open spaces, and experience life outdoors,
visit with goats, peacocks and other animals.

My husband Elicious Scott and I also love being outside.
We met on a trail ride, married a year later in a pasture.
Even the female minister and I wore cowboy hats.
Rope tricks and a dancing pig entertained guests.
It took a man ten years younger to keep up with me.

The family legacy continues with our American Cowboy Museum,
filled with old photos, slave papers, quilts, cow horns and hides,

those hands-on items giving voice to the invisible.
I tell my family's story; the museum sings our truths.

   Dede Fox

After fourteen years as a professional model in Houston, Kansas City, and New York, Mollie Stevenson, Jr., became the matriarch of a 640-acre Texas ranch owned by her family for 140 years. She and her mother Mollie Stevenson, Sr. were the first living African-Americans included in Ft. Worth's Cowgirl Hall of Fame.

Sigfredo Anahel Hernández Palomo (circa 1980's–), artist's brother

En el Nombre de Dios, Ayúdanos

I follow the coyote until my feet
are on fire, until Fernando vomits,
falls under a pummeling sun
brutal as a gang beat-down.

Smuggler won't wait.
I become a beggar:
En el nombre de Dios
ayúdanos, ayúdanos.

Then I begin 911 cell phone calls.
Four times. My voice no longer
mine but the voice of those who
bear the unbearable.

Fernando's body that lived through
the gang's bruises and fractures,
slumps now. His artist hands
lie like fallen doves.

Twelve hours without water.
Low scrub brush, air a furnace.
Nothing, no one. Silence like a flame.
Jackrabbits and the dead of Brooks County.

Fifth call: *Please, please.*
I rock him: *Stay with me. Stay.*
Fernando lies in my arms
milky pale as a flor de izote.

    Renny Golden

After Salvadoran artist José Fernando Hernández Palomo refused to design tattoos for a major gang, he was beaten to unconsciousness. After a second beating, he and his brother, Sigfredo, gave their savings to a smuggler who abandoned them in the scorching scrub land of Brown County, Texas, where 22-year-old Fernando grew too weak to walk. He died in his big brother's arms.

En el Nombre de Dios, Ayúdanos: In the Name of God, Help Us; flor de izote: national flower of El Salvador

Sophia (21st century), Asian domestic worker

Call Me Sophia

Mistress forget to trim paper extra from the grocery list. I fold it hard with my nail so it tears clean. If I am lucky, she think she rip it like most days. I must not have paper. Ever. It is mistress rule. But I have lucky day today. On store floor, I find pencil. Still, I worry. Why mistress do different today when I shop and she swim at the gym and use her machines? Only machines I use are vacuum and "kitchen gadgets." I remember swims in the river in my home. River through this desert nobody swim in for fun. I must not say where home is. It would mean death. I fear say my name, what I am call me here. They say they keep U.S. papers for me here. But they not let me carry them. At home I carry papers. All places. They say police here never check, unless trouble. And I must not make trouble. Back home, they care about missing papers. More important than missing people. Where my home papers now? Who have them? They say my father sell me because he lose cock fights. They like me. I am strong, and young, and pretty. And I speak English. Pretty good, yes? If I make trouble they hurt family. And send me to job for bad girls. This job not so bad. They give me good clothes to work, food and a room behind house. I afraid I never see my family again. I not get here on foot or in dark truck. I must not say if I take boat, or train, or plane. It is dangerous. You can believe, too many people squeeze me. Today mistress do other thing after she swim, and shower, and put makeup on face. Today I take bus, even with groceries. Mistress say use cloth bags. They are strong. You never throw away. She say, "We must care for the earth." I am at bus stop now. Sun is hot, hot today. Lizards on the wall like hot. I do not. I like to watch lizards. This paper gone, almost both sides. I miss one bus so I can finish this. Maybe I not have another lucky day, extra paper, found pencil, and busy mistress. When bus come again, I leave paper on bench for you to find. Do not tell mistress. Please.

Caroline A. LeBlanc

Human trafficking is a hidden form of modern slavery on just about every continent. Its victims are largely invisible. My experience one evening in an Asian restaurant with an obsequious adolescent male waiter, also Asian, made me remember reports, fictions and non-fiction accounts about human trafficking and modern slavery. I wondered if this young man was here by choice, and under promised conditions. This poem is in the voice of one of these souls, a young woman trapped in the American Southwest.

Southwest misfit (2012)

Devil Girl

"There goes that devil girl," they would always say.
Born to a drunk mama during the worst squall they could ever
      remember.
The devil wasn't in me,
but nothing normal was.
I was of the desert and it was of me.
Sharp and chiseled
I would come from the sagebrush with scorpions in my pockets
and lizards on my shoulders.
I had the plains in my eyes and the wind in my blood.
Anyone could see that.
But not knowing how to talk to geography,
people just stepped around me like a tree in the road,
a rock in the path,
an inconsequential part of their life that was there
whether they wanted it or not.

It was weeks before anyone noticed I was gone.
But one day they felt that something was missing,
there was an empty space that should be filled.
They were not sad because it was just the impermanence of things.
One day there was sun, the next there was rain.
One day I was there, the next I was not.
So they symbolized this bit of life and taught it to their children.
And for generations when anything went missing,
something that was suddenly gone like a box of nails or a pair of
      gloves,
they would always say, "There goes that devil girl."

    Lynn C. Reynolds

This speaker is a Southwest misfit, one of the people who identify with the land and not people.

Zozobra/Old Man Gloom (1920–), marionette effigy

Zozobra's Elegy

I'm built of paper, cloth and wood, and wear
a long, white robe; my hair is tinted green,
my eyes are glowing red. On stage, I scare

with flailing arms, horrific moans — a scene
commanding roars from frenzied crowds who wait
for fire; the loud crescendo, all chanting

"Burn Him!" for Fiestas de Santa Fe
begins with me, as I am Old Man Gloom.
The Box of Gloom, stuffed with worries, will stay

with me, the macabre image of doom,
an effigy set to collapse in fire,
as spirited dancers surround my tomb.

Yet pyrotechnics instill little fear;
I'll take all your troubles for one more year.

    Christine Wenk-Harrison

Zozobra, or Old Man Gloom, is a 50-foot marionette, constructed each fall since 1924, to open Fiestas de Santa Fe. Spectators gather to watch his demise, as he and their troubles go up in flames.

Ornella Steiner (1964–2015), French tourist/hiker

On the Way Out

Where are you, my boys, mon Anges?
I feel like I am a speck of sand,
sinking into a thousand pieces,
far from green Burgogne,
where heat is never this heat.

When I told you to walk ahead without me,
that I would return to the trail-head,
should I have mentioned
how my head feels swollen,
how each step I am slower and fall
further from our American dream?
How the white and blue of this wide
open sky and gypsum sand
are ready to bury me?

To walk here is like sinking up-hill
the soft sands of Argeles-Sur-Mer beach.
I feel the weight of each leg —
especially the one with the knee
that always aches.
Even this wouldn't be so bad
if I had brought more water.

When you disappeared over the last dune,
I swallowed your names like rain —
David, Enzo.

White Sands, she is laughing at me,
for thinking I could capture her in photos,
wrap her up, post her on Facebook
for Reims Town Hall co-workers.

She teaches me about heat,
isolation, absence.
Now that I am alone, I understand
the suffocation of vastness.

I taste my salt in the gypsum sand.
This moonscape breathes heat.
Dunes stare at me like white windows,
soak me with empty-eyed sun.

I want to argue about water!
It is your fault, David!
It is my fault.
It is ...

Tell me, do you see the orange trail markers?
Did you make it to dry Lake Otero?
Did you put your fingers into the crust
of her Ice Age bed?
I hope you did this for me.

I am sick for thirst of water —
I want to swim in a cool place,
leave this endless moon bed, nausea.

Mon Anges, I have entered an ocean of heat,
and I only have my salt to drink.

   Vanessa Zimmer-Powell

Ornella Steiner, from Burgogne, France, died while hiking with her son and husband on the Alkali Flats in White Sands, New Mexico, August 4, 2015.

mon Anges: my angels

An Orb Spider Scolds the Poet

When you gazed at the morning moon,
how did you miss the subtlety before you,
this swaying space?
Glisten of raindrops
suspended,
> anchor of
> my body.

When I formed this web across your doorway,
I thought you would see the lines
and find another way out.
You are a poet and supposed to notice.

My web is not ripped totally to shreds.
More of a loosening, a thinning
where it connects with rock wall.
I will mend my own wound,
reweave the ragged.

This time, notice
how I feel my way
along the edge — drop, turn
and turn again. Each strand
pulling like a distant memory
from my core, becoming
tangible and clear
out here in the open.

Cyra S. Dumitru

This large, talented spider is native to South Texas and demands respect from human neighbors who cannot always see clearly beyond their own habits and habitat.

Contributor Notes and Index

Gloria Amescua, a CantoMundo fellow and Hedgebrook alumna, is the author of *Windchimes* and *What Remains*. Amescua has been published in a variety of journals and anthologies, including *di-verse-city, Kweli Journal, Texas Poetry Calendar, The Acentos Review, Pilgrimage Magazine*, and *Entre Guadalupe y Malinche: Tejanas in Literature and Art*. She has also received the Austin Poetry Society Award and the Christina Sergeyevna Award. (118, 142)

Cynthia Anderson lives in the Mojave Desert near Joshua Tree National Park. Her award-winning poems appear in numerous journals, and she is the author of five collections—*In the Mojave, Desert Dweller*, and *Shared Visions I* and *II*, and *Mythic Rockscapes* (in collaboration with photographer Bill Dahl). She co-edited the anthology *A Bird Black As the Sun: California Poets on Crows & Ravens*. (98)

Carol Alena Aronoff is a psychologist, teacher and writer with poetry in numerous literary journals and anthologies. She has published five illustrated books of poetry: *The Nature of Music, Cornsilk, Her Soup Made the Moon Weep, Blessings from an Unseen World*, and *Dreaming Earth's Body* (with paintings by Betsie Miller-Kusz). She currently resides in rural Hawaii. (22, 23, 24)

Mikki Aronoff has written and published many articles about her work in the fields of therapeutic and educational puppetry and bibliotherapy in the US, the UK, and Singapore. Her poems can also be found in *House of Cards: Ekphrastic Poetry, Rolling Sixes Sestinas: an Anthology of Albuquerque Poets*, and *3ElementsReview*. Now retired, Aronoff makes her home in Albuquerque, where she continues to string words and scribble pictures and smooch on her pooches as often as she can. (136)

Patricia Spears Bigelow, author of *Midnight Housekeeping* (River Lily Press) has recent poetry in *Texas Poetry Calendar, Voices de la Luna, San Antonio Express-News*, and *Cinco de VIA: Five Years of Poetry on the Move*. In addition to poetry, she has published nonfiction articles and a novel for young readers. (158)

Travis Blair turned to writing poetry after a lengthy career in the movie business. Author of three published books, he has poetry in literary journals throughout the U.S., England, South Africa, Australia, and India. A former President of the Dallas Poets Community, he has received two Pushcart Prize nominations. Blair has two daughters and five grandchildren; he hides from them frequently in Manhattan and Mazatlán. (140)

Christine H. Boldt, a retired librarian, has lived in Central Texas for more than thirty years. She was a Peace Corps volunteer in Nigeria in the 1960s, and lived in Italy during the 1970s. Boldt has published in *Christianity and Crisis, The Washington Post, The Dallas Morning News*, and *Working Mother*. Her poetry has appeared in *The Christian Century, Windhover, Texas Poetry Calendar*, and *The Enigmatist*. Her prize-winning poems are included in The Poetry Society of Texas' *Book of the Year* (2015) and National Federation of State Poetry Societies' *Encore* (2016). (40)

Von S. Bourland, a Texas poet, has award-winning poems in *A Galaxy of Verse, The Diplomat, Byline Magazine; Encore, Golden Words, The Muse*, and *Poets' Forum Magazine*, as well as annual publications of the Mississippi, Texas, and Arizona State Poetry Societies. Internationally, she won first place in the Kaixin Poetry Competition 2009—subject, China; poem, "Pretty Feet," later published in an English-as-a-second-language textbook printed in Australia in 2009. (70)

David Bowles has taught at the University of Texas since 1997. Recipient of awards from the American Library Association, the Texas Institute of Letters, and the Texas Associated Press, Bowles is the author of several books, including *Flower, Song, Dance: Aztec and Mayan Poetry* and *Border Lore*. His verse has appeared in *Asymptote, Translation Review, Metamorphoses, Rattle, Axolotl, Huizache, Concho River Review, BorderSenses, Texas Poetry Calendar, Amarillo Bay, Red River Review, The Thing Itself, Cybersoleil Journal, Illya's Honey* and *Parabola*. (9)

Barbara Brannon studied poetry with James Dickey at the University of South Carolina, where she earned an MA and PhD. Her poems have appeared in *Asheville Poetry Review, Cenacle, Kakalak, Light, South Carolina Review,* and *Yemassee,* among other outlets. She is a frequent contributor of travel and feature articles and is coauthor, with Kay Ellington, of the Paragraph Ranch series of Texas novels. (114, 115)

Melissa Jones Brewer, of Lubbock, Texas, holds a BA in Creative Writing from Texas Tech University and an MA in Playwriting from Boston University. She has had several plays produced in regional theaters across the country and recently began submitting her poetry. Her first published poem appeared in *Southern Poetry Review,* and two of her poems are included in *The Southern Poetry Anthology, Volume VIII: Texas*. (16, 176)

Del Cain writes poetry and prose. He leads workshops, mentors writers through programs at the Saginaw Library, does contract editing, and has judged poetry contests, including two national competitions. Cain is the author of two books of nonfiction, *Lawmen of the Old West: The Good Guys* and *Lawmen of the Old West: The Bad Guys*, as well as two books of poetry, *Songs on the Prairie Wind* and *The Voices of Christmas*. His poems have appeared in *di-verse-city, Blood and Thunder, Blue Hole, Crosstimbers,* and elsewhere. He lives in Saginaw, Texas with his wife Isabel. (96)

Joan Canby is a graduate of Vermont College of Fine Arts. She worked for thirty years in corporate America—for Hughes Aircraft, General Dynamics, Ericsson, and Nortel Networks—where she was a technical writer and then a project manager in training. Her poems have appeared in *California Quarterly, The Hawaiian Advertiser, Thema, Illya's Honey, Texas Observer* and *Forces* magazine. (71)

Amanda Chiado is an MFA graduate of California College of the Arts. Her poetry has been nominated for the Pushcart Prize and is forthcoming or appears in *Best New Poets, Witness, Cimarron Review, Fence, Eleven Eleven,* and others. Chiado currently works as the Program Coordinator for the San Benito County Arts Council; she is also an active California Poet in the Schools. Chiado's chapbook *Vitiligod: The Ascension of Michael Jackson* has just been released from Dancing Girl Press & Studio. (12, 61)

Sally Clark, a native Texan, has award-winning poetry in *Relief: A Quarterly Christian Expression Journal, Weavings, Chrysalis Reader, Alive Now, Purpose, The Binnacle, Bacopa Lit-*

erary Review, Manifest West: Even Cowboys Carry Cell Phones, Lifting the Sky: Southwestern Haiku & Haiga, four issues of Texas Poetry Calendar, and eleven gift books compiled by June Cotner and published by various publishers. She is the author of a children's book, Where's My Hug? (Ideals Children's Book/Worthy Kids Publishing, 2015). (47)

Diana L. Conces lives and writes in the heart of Texas. Her work has appeared in artlines2: Art Becomes Poetry, Texas Poetry Calendar, Best of Austin Poetry 2012-2014; in the anthologies Tic Toc and Petals in the Pan; and inside a Capitol Metro bus. (26)

Karen S. Córdova is a business woman and poet. Though she lives in California, Karen has deep roots both in Colorado and New Mexico. Much of her writing reflects love of her heritage by weaving stories about la gente of the Southwest. Her ancestors are Spanish, Native American, and a few extranjero mountain men who wandered west. Córdova's work has been published in many journals. She loves participating in formal poetry events and giving poetry presentations to the general public. Her first book, Farolito, casts a Hispano light on the dark subject of elder abuse, but also illuminates a jagged path to unexpected healing. (30, 32)

Carolyn A. Dahl was the Grand Prize winner in the 2015 Public Poetry/MFAH ekphrastic poetry competition ARTlines2. Her essays and poems have appeared in twenty-five anthologies, including Women On Poetry, Beyond Forgetting, and Goodbye, Mexico, as well as various literary journals, including Copper Nickel, Plainsongs, Camas, Hawaii Review, Colere, and Pirene's Fountain. She has poems forthcoming in The Southern Poetry Anthology, Volume VIII: Texas, Civilized Beasts, and Texas Weather. A finalist from PEN Texas in nonfiction, Dahl is the author of Transforming Fabric and Natural Impressions, and co-author of The Painted Door Opened, poems and art. (152, 172)

Margaret Dornaus, a native Oklahoman, is a freelance writer and Culinary Arts Instructor currently living in the Arkansas River Valley with a twelve-year-old cat and a dog named Chef. Winner of the Tanka Society of America's 2011 International Tanka Contest, Dornaus is widely published in international journals and anthologies, including Texas Poetry Calendar, Lifting the Sky: Southwestern Haiku & Haiga, and Red River Review. (65, 93)

Cyra S. Dumitru, certified in Poetic Medicine through The Institute of Poetic Medicine, teaches poetry writing, writing as healing, and college composition. She facilitates individual and small group healing through writing circles in a variety of community settings. Dumitru has three book-length collections of her poems: What the Body Knows, Listening to Light, and remains. (52, 198)

Susan J. Erickson's first full-length collection of poems, Lauren Bacall Shares a Limousine, recently won the Brick Road Poetry Prize. Poems from that series appear in 2River View, Crab Creek Review, The Museum of Americana, The Fourth River, Naugatuck River Review, Literal Latte, and James Franco Review. Erickson lives in Bellingham, Washington, where she helped to establish the Sue C. Boynton Poetry Walk and Contest. (153)

Nancy Fine writes from the sagebrush sea on the northwestern edge of the Great Basin. Her photos and non-fiction accounts of pioneer descendants, a stroke survivor, ranchers, and other amazing folks earned her Ruralite Magazine's 2013 Writer of the Year award. Fine enjoys the hunt for words that poetry offers; she is also working on novel-length fiction. When not wrangling words—or dust bunnies—she makes tracks with her husband Matt and the rest of their herd in the more-cows-than-people-per-acre country of arid Eastern Oregon. (104)

Dede Fox's publishing credits include *The Treasure in the Tiny Blue Tin*, a children's novel from TCU Press; nonfiction articles in *Highlights*; and two poetry books—*Confessions of a Jewish Texan* and *Postcards Home*. Her poetry has appeared in *di-verse-city, The Enigmatist, Far Out: Poems of the 60's, Poetica, Sol, A Summer's Poems, Swirl, Texas Poetry Calendar*, and *Untameable City: Poems on the Nature of Houston*. (188)

Adamarie Fuller won the inaugural Artlines/Public Poetry ekphrastic poetry competition in 2012 at the Museum of Fine Arts–Houston, as well as Honorable Mention in the Austin International Poetry Festival 2011 and *Texas Poetry Calendar* awards 2009. She has poetry in several anthologies, including *The Weight of Addition*, the Austin International Poetry Festival Anthology *di-verse-city, A Summer's Poems, The Poetry Revolt*, and the anthology of the Houston Poetry Festival. (180)

Renny Golden won the Women Writing the West Willa Literary Award 2010-11 with her poetry collection *Blood Desert: Witnesses 1820-1880,* also named a Southwest Notable Book of the Year 2012 and a Finalist for the New Mexico Book Award. Golden's publication credits include *Dogwood, Water~Stone Review, International Quarterly, Main Street Rag, Literary Review, Calyx, Borderlands: Texas Poetry Review*, and *Sin Fronteras*. (183, 190)

Lyman Grant teaches creative writing, English, and humanities at Austin Community College. He is married and the proud father of three sons. A poet since high school, Grant has a big pile of poems, some of them collected in four books and one chapbook. The most recent is *Last Work: A Meditation on the Final Paintings of Neal Adams*. (160)

Barbara Randals Gregg has poetry in *di-verse-city, The Enigmatist, Blue Hole*, the Austin Poetry Society's *Best Austin Poetry* anthology, *Wingbeats: Exercises and Practice in Poetry, Lifting the Sky: Southwestern Haiku and Haiga*, and several editions of *Texas Poetry Calendar*. She currently serves as Austin Poetry Society President. (144, 148)

Dawnell H. Griffin, writer, family historian, genealogist, and poet, is the author of several published family histories and winner of the Utah State Poetry Society Book Award in 2012, with her manuscript *On Judgment Day*. Griffin has been published in *Panorama, Utah Sings,* and *The Friend*. She is the current president of the Utah State Poetry Society. (112)

Lucy Griffith, poet and essayist, lives on a ranch along the Guadalupe River near Comfort, Texas. A Certified Master Naturalist as well as a licensed psychologist, Griffith is a member of the Writers' League of Texas. She has been published monthly in *The Texas Star* and various psychology journals. Her muse is a tractor named Ruby, and a good day is one spent outside. (171)

Nels Hanson has had poems in *Word Riot, The Oklahoma Review, Pacific Review*, and other journals. He received a 2014 Pushcart nomination in poetry, *Sharkpack Poetry Re-*

view's 2014 Prospero Prize, and a 2015 Best of the Net nomination. His fiction won the San Francisco Foundation's James D. Phelan Award, as well as Pushcart nominations in 2010, '12, and '14. (64)

Michelle Hartman is the author of two poetry collections—*Irony and Irreverence* and *Disenchanted and Disgruntled*, both from Lamar University Press. With work featured in *Langdon Review of the Arts in Texas*, Hartman has poems in more than sixty journals and thirty anthologies, both here and abroad. A native of Fort Worth, with a BS in Political Science Pre-Law from Texas Wesleyan University, she is the editor of *Red River Review*. (86, 109)

Michael Harty combines his poetry avocation with his day job as a psychoanalyst. His poems have appeared in *The Lyric, The Comstock Review, New Letters*, and elsewhere, including several editions of *Texas Poetry Calendar*. He lives and works near Kansas City. (20)

J. Todd Hawkins has poems in *AGNI, The American Literary Review, Bayou Magazine, The Louisville Review, Chiron Review, Wisconsin Review*, and elsewhere. His haiku and haiga were included in *Lifting the Sky: Southwestern Haiku and Haiga* (Dos Gatos Press). He holds an MA in Technical Communication and works as the managing editor for an educational publisher. (66, 94, 120)

Dolores Hayden is the author of *Exuberance*, celebrating several stunt pilots, including Lincoln Beachey, Harriet Quimby, Blanche Stuart Scott, and Bessie Coleman. Her previous poetry books are *American Yard* and *Nymph, Dun, and Spinner*. Recent work has appeared in *Poetry, Shenandoah, Raritan, Best American Poetry, Ecotone*, and *The Yale Review*. A poetry fellow at Djerassi and VCCA, Hayden has received awards from the Poetry Society of America and the New England Poetry Club. (110)

Fatima-Ayan Malika Hirsi writes in Arlington, Texas. She has performed in various stage productions across the state, and her work can be read in *Vagabonds, Life in 10 Minutes, Poem Your Heart Out*, Volume 1, and *Writer's Digest*. She can often be found on the sidewalks of Dallas creating spontaneous poems for passersby on her typewriter. (106)

Katherine Hoerth is the author of two poetry collections, *Goddess Wears Cowboy Boots* and *The Garden Uprooted*. The Texas Institute of Letters awarded her the Helen C. Smith Prize for the best book of poetry in 2015. Her work has been included in journals such as *Borderlands: Texas Poetry Review, Concho River Review,* and *Mezzo Cammin*. (44, 59, 60)

Ann Howells has edited *Illya's Honey* for fifteen years, recently taking it digital. Her chapbooks are *Black Crow in Flight* and *the Rosebud Diaries. Under a Lone Star,* Texas poems illustrated by Dallas artist Darrell Kirkley, was published by Village Books Press in 2016. (42, 138)

Armando P. Ibáñez is a writer, poet, professor, and filmmaker, whose award-winning documentaries include *South Texas Gentle Men of Steel—Los Padres* (2015) and *Not Broken* (2007), about the Katrina disaster. The founder and President of Pluma Pictures Inc., a non-profit film production company, he earned an MFA from The American Film Institute. Ibáñez, a Dominican friar, serves as Director of the Radio-Television-Film Program

(RTF) and Assistant Professor at Texas A&M University-Kingsville, where he teaches screenwriting, producing and directing. (7)

Aletha Irby is grateful to have been granted this time, on this planet, to spend with the English language. She has had poems in *Epiphany, Shot Glass Journal, Texas Poetry Calendar,* and *VOLT*. Aletha is currently working on an epic; she lives in Austin, Texas. (116)

Marcelle H. Kasprowicz, a native of France, has an MA from the University of Texas–Austin. Writing in both English and French, she translates her French poems into English. Kasprowicz has multiple publication credits, as well as several poetry prizes. She is the author of five collections: *Organza Skies: Poems from the Davis Mountains, Children Playing with Leopards, Out of Light Darkness, Her Blue Touch,* and *Le Silence de la Lumière*. (18)

Jan La Roche, has been editor of *Oberon Poetry Magazine* for three years. Her work has appeared in *Möbius, Paumanok: Poems and Pictures of Long Island, Paumanok II,* and *Earth's Daughters: Shift*. Co-author of *25 Year, Poems, and Drawings* with her husband, Jef Bravata, La Roche is currently working on a new poetry collection, *Through the Loupe*. (126)

Gayle Lauradunn's debut poetry collection *Reaching for Air* was a finalist for Best First Book of Poetry at the Texas Institute of Letters. Co-organizer of the first National Women's Multicultural Poetry Festival held at the University of Massachusetts, Amherst, Lauradunn served as an editor of *Chomo-Uri,* a women's literary and arts journal. Her second collection received Honorable Mention for the May Sarton New Hampshire Poetry Prize from Bauhan Publishing. (135)

Jim LaVilla-Havelin is the author of four books of poetry, including *Counting* (Pecan Grove Press, 2010). *West,* a new book of poems, is being published by Wings Press in 2017. Poet, teacher, and community arts activist, LaVilla-Havelin is the coordinator of National Poetry Month in San Antonio and the Poetry Editor for the *San Antonio Express-News*. (174)

Caroline LeBlanc, with an MFA in Creative Writing from Spalding University, is the author of the chapbook, *Smokey Ink and a Touch of Honeysuckle* (Oiseau Press, 2010), as well as essays and prize-winning poetry published in the U.S. and abroad. LeBlanc contributes to the Poetry Matters blog, staffed by Spalding University alumni. From 2013–15 she served as the American Military Family Museum's Writer in Residence; she hosts a regular writing salon for women veterans. A founding member of the Albuquerque Apronistas Collective of women artists, LeBlanc has won prizes in numerous group shows. (192)

Gordon L. Magill is a journalist, writing teacher, exhibit writer, freelancer, and poet. He has worked at *The Washington Evening Star* and the *Washington Post,* and has taught writing at the Institute of American Indian Arts in Santa Fe, New Mexico, as well as in public high schools. Author of numerous published articles and short stories, Magill has recent work in *The Enigmatist* and *Blue Hole*. (128)

Wade Martin is co-editor of the *Texas Poetry Calendar* and a 2014 Pushcart nominee for a poem in *Illya's Honey*. He has recent work in *Perfume River Poetry Review, Freshwater Poetry Magazine, Bird's Thumb,* and online at Silver Birch Press. Martin's thoughts on the writing life can be read at *SPANK the CARP* and the Writers' League of Texas blog *Scribe*. (88, 100, 106)

Darla McBryde makes her home in Alpine, Texas, after previous chapters in Houston and Austin. A previous feature for the Houston Library's Public Poetry program, McBryde was chosen two years in a row for the Houston performance poetry group "Word Around Town." A Pushcart Nominee, she has also received the Houston Poetry Fest's Lorene Pouncey Award. Her work has appeared in *Texas Poetry Calendar, San Pedro River Review, Illya's Honey, Cenizo Journal,* and elsewhere. McBryde has published four chapbooks. (184)

Anne McCrady has numerous publication credits, including *Langdon Review of the Arts in Texas, Borderlands: Texas Poetry Review, The Texas Review, The Texas Observer, Texas Poetry Calendar, Her Texas,* and *The Southern Poetry Anthology, Volume VIII: Texas*. Her poetry collections include *Along Greathouse Road, Under a Blameless Moon,* and *Letting Myself In*. A co-founder of Texas Poets Podcast and Northeast Texas Poetry in Schools, McCrady posts weekly news-related poems at Poet with a Press Pass. She lives in Tyler, Texas, where she runs InSpiritry. (78, 178)

David Meischen has recent poems in *Assaracus, Borderlands, Naugatuck River Review, San Pedro River Review, Southern Poetry Review,* and *Talking Writing*. Winner of the Writers League of Texas manuscript award in Mainstream Fiction (2011) and the Talking Writing Prize for Short Fiction (2012), David has an agent promoting his novel in stories. A chapter of his memoir in progress is forthcoming in *The Gettysburg Review*. Co-founder of Dos Gatos Press, David served as co-editor of *Wingbeats* and *Wingbeats II*, collections of poetry writing exercises. (10)

John Milkereit is a rotating equipment engineer working in Houston, Texas. His chapbooks are *Home & Away* and *Paying Admissions;* his book-length collection, *A Rotating Equipment Engineer is Never Finished* (Ink Brush Press, 2015). Milkereit is finishing a low-residency MFA program at the Rainier Writing Workshop in Tacoma, Washington. (166)

Paula Miller has had a long time interest in Native healing practices and herbal medicines. She has been writing poetry for many years, most recently about changes in imagery that come with moving to New Mexico. She has been published in *Malpais Review* and *Bosque Rhythms*. (162)

Michael Montlack, author of the poetry collection *Cool Limbo*, served as editor of the Lambda Finalist essay anthology *My Diva*. He has recent work in *Cimarron Review, Barrow Street, The Cortland Review, Hotel Amerika, The Gay and Lesbian Review,* and other journals and anthologies. (168)

Rachel Anna Neff has written poetry since elementary school and has notebooks full of half-written novels. She earned her doctorate in Spanish literature from the University of California–Riverside and is currently working on her MFA from the University of Texas at El Paso. Her erasure poem "Night Meeting" is forthcoming in the Hyacinth Girl Press anthology *Bye Bye Bukowski*. (134)

Katherine Durham Oldmixon has recent poems in *Borderlands: Texas Poetry Review*, *Solstice Literary Magazine*, *Improbable Worlds: An Anthology of Texas and Louisiana Poets*, *Lifting the Sky*, and *Texas Poetry Calendar*, as well as her chapbook *Water Signs*. Co-director of Poetry at Round Top and a senior poetry editor for *Tupelo Quarterly*, Oldmixon is professor and chair of English at Huston-Tillotson University in Austin, Texas. (58, 130).

Christa Pandey has been widely published since she moved to Austin. As a German immigrant herself, she became interested in the immigration saga of the nineteenth century. Her poems are collected in three chapbooks—*Southern Seasons*, *Maya*, and *Hummingbird Wings*. Recent publication credits include *Texas Poetry Calendar*, the *Poetry @ Round Top Anthology*, *Naugatuck River Review*, and online at Silver Birch Press. (84)

Elina Petrova lived in Ukraine until 2007, where she worked worked in engineering management. Petrova has many Russian and Ukrainian publication credits, as well as a book of Russian-language poems. Currently working in a Houston law firm, she has recent work in *Texas Poetry Calendar*, *The Texas Review*, *FreeFall*, *Voices de la Luna*, *Harbinger Asylum*, *Illya's Honey*, *Melancholy Hyperbole*, *Panoply*, the anthologies of the Houston and Austin poetry festivals, and *Untameable City*. *Aching Miracle*, her first book of poetry in English, had its official release in September 2015. (54)

Anjela Villarreal Ratliff is a writing workshop presenter. Her work has appeared in various publications, including *Cantos al Sexto Sol: An Anthology of Aztlanahuac Writing*, *Lifting the Sky: Southwestern Haiku & Haiga*, *The Enigmatist*, *Blue Hole*, *Texas Poetry Calendar*, and *Australian Latino Press*. A Texas native, she lives in Austin. (36, 150)

C. Samuel Rees has been featured in *Fairy Tale Review*, *Permafrost*, *Raw Paw*, *Borderlands: Texas Poetry Review*, *Pithead Chapel*, *JMWW*, and *Row Home Lit*. He has poems upcoming in the anthology *The Dead Animal Handbook* (University of Hell Press), and *Fairy Tale Review*'s Translucent Issue. Currently he works as an educator in Austin, TX, where he writes poetry and reads about deserts. (132)

Charlotte Renk is the author of three poetry collections — *These Holy Hungers: Secret Yearnings from an Empty Cup*, *Solidago: An Altar to Weeds*, and *The Tenderest Petal Hears*, co-winner of the 2014 Blue Horse Press Chapbook Award. Her poetry has appeared in journals such as *Kalliope*, *Concho River Review*, *The Sow's Ear Poetry Review*, *Southwest Review*, and *Langdon Review of the Arts in Texas*, as well as anthologies such as *The Southern Poetry Anthology, Volume VIII: Texas*, and *Her Texas*. (164)

Lynn Reynolds wrote many poems while a member of the Houston Poetry Society, the Poetry Society of Texas and Poets, Ink. A juried poet at the 2012 and 2015 Houston Poetry Fests, she has poetry in *From Hide and Horn: A Sesquicentennial Anthology of Texas Poets*, *Texas Poetry Calendar*, and *Untameable City*. (194)

Sharon Rhutasel-Jones taught for over half a century. Since retiring, she has published two books — *Living by Ear: Memoir of a Wayward Teacher* and *The Teacher Who Learned from Cats*. She is currently working on a bilingual picture book of haiku for children. (62)

Ann Ritter has work in *Adanna, Earth First, The Southern Poetry Anthology, Volume V: Georgia, Gathered: Contemporary Quaker Poets,* and forthcoming in *Elements.* Her fiction, essays and poetry have appeared in *Charleston Magazine, Confrontation, Earth's Daughters, THEMA, Georgia Journal,* and *Like a Summer Peach: Sunbright Poems and Old Southern Recipes.* Ritter has studied in the summer writing program at Bennington College, Vermont, and received an artist-initiated grant from the Georgia Council for the Arts in fiction and poetry. A former business journalist, she serves as a communication instructor at Georgia State University, Atlanta. (156)

Barbara Robidoux has published two books of poetry — *Waiting for Rain* and *Migrant Moon.* Her poetry has appeared in *Santa Fe Literary Review, Más Tequila Review, Off the Coast, Ribbons, Lynx,* and *Hinchas de Poesia.* Her fiction has appeared in the *Yellow Medicine Review, Denver Quarterly,* and *Santa Fe Literary Review,* and her collection of linked short stories *Sweetgrass Burning : Stories from the Rez* was published in 2016 by BlueHand Books. She lives in Santa Fe, where she is an MFA candidate in Creative Writing at the Institute of American Indian Arts, where she also works. (182)

Susan Rooke has recent poems in *A Year of Being Here, Texas Poetry Calendar, San Pedro River Review,* and the anthologies *Pushing the Envelope: Epistolary Poems* and *Grit, Gravity and Grace: New Poems about Medicine and Healthcare.* A three-time Pushcart Prize nominee and a Best of the Net nominee, she lives in the country outside of Thorndale, Texas. (72)

Jan Seale, 2012 Texas Poet Laureate, is a resident of the Rio Grande Valley of Texas. Her writings include nine books of poetry, two of short fiction, and three of nonfiction. She is the recipient of seven PEN Syndicated Fiction Project awards. Her latest books are *The Parkinson Poems, Appearances: Stories,* and *Nature, Nurture, Neither.* (34)

Linda Simone, poet and watercolorist, moved to San Antonio, Texas from New York. Her poems have been nominated for a Pushcart Prize and have appeared in more than eighty journals, including *Adanna* and *Carnival Magazine,* and in numerous anthologies, including *Cradle Songs* and *Lavanderia: A Mixed Load of Women, Wash, and Word.* Her chapbooks include *Archeology,* and *Cow Tippers.* She is proud to be listed in the San Antonio Poet Source. (124)

Jennifer Smith has been published in several anthologies, including *Love Notes* and *Lifting the Sky.* An English Professor in Los Angeles, she is currently working on her Doctorate in Education from UCLA.She is a part of the Puente Program, which emphasis Latino literature and culture in a transfer program for underrepresented students. (8)

Sandi Stromberg served as guest editor of *Untameable City: Poems on the Nature of Houston,* the latest poetry anthology from Mutabilis Press. Her poetry has appeared in *Texas Poetry Calendar, Borderlands: Texas Poetry Review, Red River Review, Illya's Honey,* and *Colere,* among others, as well as in the anthologies *TimeSlice, The Weight of Addition,* and *Improbable Worlds, Crossing Lines,* and *Goodbye, Mexico.* She has work forthcoming in *Civilized Beasts* and *Texas Weather Anthology.* A Pushcart nominee, she has been a juried poet in the Houston Poetry Fest eight times. (122)

Susan Terris is the author of six books of poetry, fifteen chapbooks, and three artist's books, most recently *Ghost of Yesterday: New & Selected Poems*. A poem of hers from *Field* appeared in *Pushcart Prize XXXI*. Her chapbook *Memos* is new from Omnidawn. A poem from *Memos* was selected by Sherman Alexie to be included in *Best American Poetry 2015*. Terris serves as editor of *Spillway Magazine*. (101)

Larry D. Thomas, a member of the Texas Institute of Letters, served as the 2008 Texas Poet Laureate. He is the author of several collections of poetry, most recently *As If Light Actually Matters: New & Selected Poems*. (154)

Mary Torregrossa has poetry in *Wide Awake: Poets of Los Angeles and Beyond* and *Poems of Arrival*, ShinPei Takeda's project for the Inscription Installation at the New Americans Museum in San Diego. Her poems in memoriam are included in Juan Felipe Herrera's project *The Most Incredible and Biggest Poem on Unity in the World*, as well as *Lament for the Dead*, honoring victims of gun violence. Poems also appear in *Like a Girl*, *Lummox*, *Altadena Poetry Review*, and elsewhere. A winner of the Arroyo Arts Collective Poetry In The Windows project, Torregrossa was named Newer Poet of Los Angeles XIV. (186)

Alana Torrez is a former spy, world traveler, and reckless poet cleverly disguised as a bespectacled office worker. Her day moves include responding to e-mails and entering grades; she spices up her night moves by working towards an MFA in Poetry at Texas State University. A poem of hers was published in the 2015 *Texas Poetry Calendar*. (28)

Leticia A. Urieta, a Tejana writer from Austin, Texas, is a graduate of Agnes Scott College and a fiction candidate in the MFA program at Texas State University. She won Agnes Scott's Academy of American Poets' prize in 2009, and her work has appeared in *Cleaver*, *Texas Poetry Calendar*, and *Black Heart*. Urieta is using her love of Texas history and passion for research to write a historical novel about the role of Mexican soldaderas in Texas' war with Mexico. (38, 74)

Sylvia Riojas Vaughn has poetry in *Triadæ Magazine*, *Lifting the Sky: Southwestern Haiku & Haiga*, *Texas Poetry Calendar*, *HOUSEBOAT*, *Red River Review*, *The Applicant*, *Diálogo*, *Label Me Latina/o*, *Somos en escrito: The Latino Literary Online Magazine*, *Desde Hong Kong: Poets in Conversation with Octavio Paz*, and numerous other anthologies and journals. She has been selected as a Houston Poetry Fest Juried Poet three times. A Pushcart Prize and Best of the Net nominee, Vaughn belongs to the Dallas Poets Community. (68, 76)

Loretta Diane Walker is a three-time Pushcart Prize nominee. Her work has appeared in a number of journals and anthologies. Walker was named the 2015 "Statesman in the Arts" by the Heritage Council of Odessa. She has published three collections of poetry, most recently *In This House* and *Word Ghetto*, winner of the 2011 Bluelight Press Book Award (50, 82)

Jimmie Ware, freelance writer, performance poet, and workshop facilitaror, has numerous publication credits, including *F Magazine*, *BlazeVox*, *Vox Poetica*, *Blast Furnace*, *The Good Men Project*, and *No More Silent Cries*. Formerly the host of Poetic Soul and a radio personality on KFAT 92.9, both in Anchorage, Ware has written for nearly twenty-five years. She resides in Phoenix with her lovely daughter Nicole. (85)

Mobi Warren is a high school math teacher, poet, and citizen scientist particularly entranced by insects and other small beings of the Southwest. Her poems have been published in several anthologies and she is the translator of several books by the Vietnamese Buddhist monk Thich Nhat Hanh, including *Old Path White Clouds*. (3)

Christine Wenk-Harrison has had poems in *Texas Poetry Calendar* and *Lifting the Sky: Southwestern Haiku & Haiga*. Her work has also appeared in *Blue Hole, Illya's Honey, Red River Review*, and on buses as part of San Antonio's *Poetry on the Move* project. She lives in Lago Vista, Texas. (195)

Marilyn Westfall has recent poetry in *Pilgrimage Magazine, Right Hand Pointing, Southwestern American Literature, Illya's Honey, Red River Review, Gravel Magazine, Mezzo Cammin, Concho River Review*, and *The Southern Poetry Anthology, Volume VIII: Texas*. Westfall holds a PhD in English from Texas Tech. (102, 146)

Allyson Whipple is a student in the online MFA program through the University of Texas at El Paso. She is the author of the chapbook *We're Smaller Than We Think We Are* and co-editor of the *Texas Poetry Calendar*. Whipple teaches at Austin Community College. (92)

Neal Whitman began to write poetry in 2005 in transition into retirement after thirty-seven years in academic medicine. When he retired in 2008 as Professor Emeritus at the University of Utah School of Medicine, he added haiku to his repertoire and tanka in 2011. Whitman and his wife Elaine live in Pacifiic Grove, Calfiornia. Both have been volunteer docents at poet Robinson Jeffers' Tor House in nearby Carmel and volunteers at the Hospice of the Central Coast. In recital, they combine his poetry and her Native American flute and photography. (48)

Liza Wolff-Francis has an MFA in Creative Writing from Goddard College. She was co-director for the 2014 Austin International Poetry Festival and a member of the 2008 Albuquerque Poetry Slam Team. Her ekphrastic poem after El Anatsui's sculpture *Seepage* is displayed adjacent to the sculpture in Austin's Blanton Art Museum. Wolff-Francis has recent work in *Poetry Pacific, Edge, Border Senses,* the anthology *Twenty,* and various blogs. Her chapbook is *Language of Crossing,* poems about the Mexico-U.S. border. (56)

Robert Wynne earned his MFA in Creative Writing from Antioch University. A former co-editor of *Cider Press Review*, he has published six chapbooks, and three book-length collections of poetry, most recently *Self-Portrait as Odysseus* (Tebot Bach Press, 2011). Wynne has won numerous prizes, and his poetry has appeared in magazines and anthologies throughout North America. He lives in Burleson, Texas with his wife and two rambunctious dogs. (15)

Vanessa Zimmer-Powell was the winner of a Rick Steves Haiku Award and honors at the 2013 Austin International Poetry Festival. Recent work has appeared or is forthcoming in *The Weekly Avocet, Avocet: A Journal of Nature Poems, Borderlands: Texas Poetry Review, Ekphrasis, Untameable City, Texas Poetry Calendar, San Pedro River Review,* and *The Chaffey Review*. (196)

Editors

Cindy Huyser's chapbook, *Burning Number Five: Power Plant Poems*, was a co-winner of the 2014 Blue Horse Press Poetry Chapbook contest. Twice nominated for a Pushcart Prize, her poetry has been published in a variety of journals and anthologies, most recently *Untameable City, Blue Hole,* and the anthology of the 2015 Houston Poetry Festival. Huyser co-edited the *Texas Poetry Calendar* from 2009 to 2014. https://cindyhuyser.wordpress.com (90)

Scott Wiggerman's *Leaf and Beak: Sonnets*, a finalist for the Helen C. Smith Memorial Award for Best Book of Poetry with the Texas Institute of Letters, is preceded by two previous collections — *Presence,* and *Vegetables and Other Relationships.* Wiggerman has served as editor of several books, including *Wingbeats: Exercises & Practice in Poetry, Lifting the Sky: Southwestern Haiku & Haiga,* and *Wingbeats II*. Recent poems have appeared in *Chrysanthemum, Red Earth Review, Frogpond, Borderlands: Texas Poetry Review, Naugatuck River Review,* and many other publications. He is co-founder and chief editor for Dos Gatos Press. http://swig.tripod.com (80)

Artist

Robert Lentz, OFM, is an iconographer with a remarkable life story. A Byzantine Rite Catholic, born in rural Colorado, Brother Lentz spent six years with the Franciscan friars of the Cincinnati Province. In 1975, he entered the Russian Orthodox Church; he studied iconography at Holy Transfiguration Monastery in Brookline, Massachusetts. As an iconographer, Brother Lentz has expanded his subject matter to include icons of people who have struggled for justice and peace — figures such as Ghandi, Martin Luther King, and Harvey Milk. For more about Brother Lentz, his inspiring life and work, see robertlentz.com. A number of his icons are available at trinitystores.com

Foreword

Carmen Tafolla, 2015 State Poet Laureate of Texas, is the author of more than twenty books and a Professor of Transformative Children's Literature at the University of Texas at San Antonio. Tafolla's work has been published in English, Spanish, German, French, and Bengali, and has been recognized by the National Association for Chicano Studies for "giving voice to the peoples and cultures of this land." She has received many recognitions, including the Américas Award, five International Latino Book Awards, and the Art of Peace, for work which contributes to peace, justice, and human understanding. http://www.carmentafolla.com (4, 6)

Index of Personae

Albert, John David (mountain man), 32
Ancestral Puebloan potter, 9
Ancestral Puebloan women, 10
Angel, Paula (murderer), 56
Angelina (Hasinai interpreter), 28
Anole (lizard), 3
Asian domestic worker, 192
Austin, Mary Hunter (nature writer), 92

Barr, Candy (stripper, dancer), 180
Billy the Kid (outlaw), 144
Brown, Hoodoo (outlaw leader), 85

Cabeza de Vaca, Álvar Núñez (explorer), 18, 132
Cactus, 47
Calamity Jane (frontierswoman), 59
Canary, Martha Jane (frontierswoman), 59
Cárdenas, García López de (Spanish conquistador), 15
Castañón Villanueva, Andrea (innkeeper), 34
Castello, Thomas Elwin (security officer, alien theorist), 166
Castillo Maldonado, Alonso del (explorer), 16
Chavez, Brian Joseph (Cochiti mercy-killer), 182
Chipeta (Native rights advocate), 112
Cochise (Apache leader), 54
Colter, Mary (architect), 146
Conkling, Margaret Badenoch Vear (teacher), 115
Conkling, Roscoe Platt (explorer, author), 114
Corbett, Jim (activist, environmentalist), 164
Corn Maidens (Hopi legend), 8
Cortés, Carlos (faux bois artist), 174
Cortez Lira, Gregorio (farmer, folk hero), 88

Dobie, J. Frank (writer and folklorist), 140
Dorsey, Marvin L. (rancher), 186

Earp, Wyatt (frontiersman), 116

Esparza, Enrique (Alamo witness), 36
Evans, William (carnival operator), 120

Flipper, Henry Ossian (soldier), 82

Gavino Doporto, Dolores (widow and legend), 78
Gilpin, Laura (photographer), 153
Gladney, Edna (children's rights campaigner), 138
Goodloe, Sid (rancher), 172
Gray, Eunice (brothel and hotel owner), 86
Guenther, Carl Hilmar (pioneer miller), 84

Hanged man, 64
Hopi cotton picker/weaver, 7

Japanese internees, 130
Jingu, Miyoshi (hostess, actress), 124
Jones, Helen Ruth (grandmother), 176
Judd, Donald (artist), 154

Kay (from a Robert Earl Keen song), 160
King, Silvia (slave), 52
Kirkland, Vance Hall (painter), 152

La Llorona (legendary ghost), 12
Lanker, Lynda (portrait artist), 178
Lea, Tom C., III (muralist/artist), 134
Leroy, Kitty (gambler), 60, 61
Locklear, Ormer (daredevil stunt pilot), 110
Loretto Chapel staircase, 70

MacDonald, Peter (Navajo code talker, politician), 128
Madam Candelaria (innkeeper), 34
Magers, Judy Ann (burro rider), 171
Magoffin, Susan Shelby (diarist), 40
Martínez, Antonio José (priest, educator, leader), 62
McJunkin, George (cowboy), 104
Meem, John Gaw, IV (architect), 136
Migrant mother, 118, 150

Misfit, 194
Mosey, Phoebe Ann (sharpshooter), 101
Moth, polyphemous 3
Mules (from a Cather novel), 48

Naduah (Comanche captive), 58
Neill, Hyman G. (outlaw leader), 85
Nez, Chester (Navajo code talker), 126
Nicks, Stephanie Lynn "Stevie" (singer/songwriter), 168
Norris, J. Frank (Baptist preacher), 109

O'Keeffe, Georgia (artist), 156, 158
Oakley, Annie (sharpshooter), 101
Old Joe (horse), 72
Old Man Gloom (marionette effigy), 195
Oppenheimer, Robert (physicist), 132
Orb spider, 198
Orejas de Conejo (Native American leader), 26

Palomo, Sigfredo Anahel Hernández (artist's brother), 190
Parker, Cynthia Ann (Comanche captive), 58
Pecos Bill (tall tale cowboy), 42
Phoenix Indian School, 106
Pino, Gabrielita (curandera), 162
Place, Etta (brothel and hotel owner), 86
Polyphemous moth, 3

Quilt, 148

Rabbit Ears (Native American leader), 26
Reeves, Bass (Deputy U.S. Marshal), 96
Ridley, Sylvia (Choctaw woman), 94
Roberts, Brushy Bill (outlaw), 144
Roberts, Ollie P. (outlaw), 144
Rogers, Eugene F. (merchant), 71
Romero, Maria Isabel (Conversa/Crypto-Jew), 22, 23, 24

Salsig, E.B. (lumber manager), 66
Scorpion, 135

Settler, West Texas, 102
Slue-Foot Sue (tall tale daredevil), 44
Slusher, Juanita Dale (stripper, dancer), 180
Smith, Rebecca "Becky" (rancher), 184
Soldaderas, 38
Sophia (Asian domestic worker), 192
Southwest misfit, 194
Starr, Belle (outlaw), 65
Starr, Myra Maybelle Shirley Reed (outlaw), 65
Steiner, Ornella (French tourist/hiker), 196
Stevenson, Mollie Taylor, Jr. (rancher, cowgirl), 188
Swift Fox (Paiute fugitive), 98

Tabor, Elizabeth McCourt "Baby Doe" (society patron), 93
Tejano guitarist, 142
Tlochtli player, 6
Turk, The (Native American slave and guide), 20

Urrea, Teresa (folk healer), 74, 76

Vigil, Maria Ysidora (Hispano mountain man's partner), 30

We'wha (Zuni Two-Spirit), 80
West Texas settler, 102
West, Emily D. (folk heroine), 50
White Singing Bird (Native rights advocate), 112
White, W.A. (photographer), 68
Wickenburg, Henry (prospector), 90
Williams, Carrie Elizabeth Zimpleman (Texas transplant), 122
Willie Boy (Paiute fugitive), 98
Wolf (Cochiti boy), 183

Yanaguana (Payaya woman/spirit), 4
Yellow Rose of Texas (folk heroine), 50

Zavala, Adina Amelia de (preservationist), 100
Zozobra (marionette effigy), 195

www.ingramcontent.com/pod-product-compliance
Lightning Source LLC
Chambersburg PA
CBHW050633300426
44112CB00012B/1774